# BELIEVE IN YOUR SOUL

Vanessa LeMaistre

# TABLE OF CONTENT

# DEDICATION

To God, the Creator, the Source, the one who I have called my Father since I was 7. This is for you. My Mother, and to grandma, whom I love and appreciate with all my heart. Thank you for all that you have sacrificed and instilled within me. Thank you for your love and kindness. To my beautiful son Kamden in heaven... thank you for choosing me. Thank you for all that you have taught me and are still teaching me. Thank you for inspiring your momma bear forever. To Nadia in heaven, hey girl hey! Thank you for your soul, your friendship, and impact in my life. And to every single soul that has been a part of my story and journey...

## PRAYER

Just so you know, every single time I sat down to write this book, I would pray to the Holy Spirit first. (I'm not even religious, more so spiritual), but I would literally ask It to help guide every word and sentence and structure so this book could have meaning for those who felt so inclined to pick it up.

This book is channeled to some degree. How you choose to use it will be channeled as well. I trust that right now as you are reading this line, you are being guided by Spirit.

Even if it's just a piece of this book that you, the reader, reads... I pray that the Holy Spirit has guided you to this for reasons beyond my knowing to be a light in your life. I ask the Holy Spirit to have every soul who finds this book, for this to help them in dire times of need; whether it be that it's hard for you to get up in the morning, it's hard for you to keep going, it's hard for you to find the joy in life, or to even find the joy in you. I pray that it is helpful when you don't know why you are here in this planet in the form that you came here as with all of your unique qualities. I pray that you are open to all that this piece of treasure has in store for you. I pray that it inspires you, not only for personal gain but so much that you are then inspired to inspire others... even if it is with a smile or a high five. Or if it's you moving forward with your life taking the time to inspire others when you can.

Come along and join in on this spiritual yet nonconventional book that will hopefully inspire you to show up as your authentic self and believe in your Soul. ~ XO

## DISCLOSURE

This is not a memoir, and this is not your typical "self-help" book. This book is written very conversationally. In place of the word "realize," I usually say **"real-eyes,"** to emphasize Self-development and transformation. The point is to make it as easy as a read as possible where any 17- year- old and any 90- year- old can read it and gain something out of it. Please by any means, if you feel inspired to, give copies away to the homeless, those in need, those on drugs and any lost soul you know.

The goal is inspiration here. I have gone through a lot- some of life's hardest hands to be dealt and I know that if I could get through it, anyone else can get through hard times.

I'm not saying I know it all, but I am hoping people can gain something substantial out of this if nothing else.

And I'm not saying that you had to have gone through a lot to read this book, but you are human, and being human can be fucking hard.

I believe human beings are the most powerful and intelligent beings that have ever existed. The question is, who among us has what it takes to unlock their full potential? Who has what it takes to co-create with what the Universe has already written for you? Who has what it takes to chase the dreams stirring up in their hearts, facing all the fears, failures and challenges that may come up? I'm not talking about the courage to jump out of a plane and skydive, but the courage to overcome personal fears like "I'm not good enough," or "I'll never succeed," or "they won't want someone like me..." "I suck." In this book, I'm here to tell you that the person who can overcome these fears is YOU.

I'm guessing because this book found its way in your hands, you're ready to have an open mind or already have one. Rather than instructing you on what to do, I intend to present new ways to think about things.

A lot of this book is channeled between my son Kamden and I as well. He is very much a part of this book.

Every chapter ends with positive affirmations/practices you can incorporate in your daily life.

# PROLOGUE

My story is pretty crazy. I finished my first draft 8 years ago and my book is all about overcoming things and believing in your soul. I had already overcome pretty big adversities, and this is initially why I wanted to inspire others. But then, once I finished my first draft, I went through one of the most difficult things anyone could ever imagine going through. Something I never thought would happen to me, something inconceivably catastrophic. Probably the hardest thing to go through humanly possible. I gave birth to my beautiful son named Kamden. He was the biggest blessing in my entire life. His soul was so pristine and so divine. However, 3 weeks after his birth, we discovered he had a rare fatal disease called Zellweger's syndrome and the doctors said he would live for 3 months max! Knowing that I would only have a short time with my precious angel, I gave him all the love I had within me and my heart. My best friend Nadia and I gave him so much love, he lived for a full 9 months. He got a lot of love from others as well. Yes, this was a special time in my life, probably the best times ever were spent with him. And while I knew it was good while these moments would last, I knew at the moment of his prognosis that I would have to believe in my soul more than ever before in my entire life. I also knew that my book was Not completed as this would be the biggest obstacle one would ever have to overcome. Three years later, here I am rewriting this book, this time channeling through the voice of my precious beautiful king- Kamden Lee Efevberha. He is so much a part of my life forevermore and a part of this project that I felt compelled to include him. Thank you for taking the time to read Believe in Your Soul.

# BACKGROUND

Channeled between Kamden and Vanessa in italicized:

*"My mommy grew up as a beautiful girl. But she never felt beautiful. She had too many things happen to her in her past, even from the time of her birth. Her daddy abandoned her when her mom and him split in the middle of her pregnancy. She grew up later to find him when she turned 30, which is when she discovered she was the only one out of all 10 kids he had around the world that he chose not to ever communicate with. She even discovered that she had a brother, the only child he chose to raise in his house, 6 months younger than her. She also discovered her dad was half Lebanese, discovering a side to her she never knew about. She knew her mom was half French, but she thought the rest of her bloodline was black from Haiti. She was wrong.*

*When Vanessa was 4-years-old, her mother had told her about not letting anyone touch her in her private parts. But because her mom was a single parent and had to work overtime all the time, she had many babysitters. A 17-year-old boy pinned her up against a bathroom sliding door and molested her. She blacked out and ran home crying to her mom to tell her what happened. She said 'mommy, mommy Patrick touched me.' Her mom stared at her blankly. She could not process what had happened to her precious Vanessa. This in turn taught Vanessa that it was okay for people to touch her whenever they wanted. And so, until Vanessa was 14, countless people, boys and girls and men molested her."*

At the age of 25, I began my healing process, and it was very intense. For the first time in my life, I was looking at the extreme trauma I endured since birth. My journey had been pretty expansive in the sense that my soul had been pushed to its limits. I have had to overcome those limits, numerous times. And still, I move forward.

As a child, I was always independent. I had to fend for myself without my dad in the picture and with my mother constantly working. I started working when I was 14-years-old, so I knew all about how to be independent. However, as I began my healing journey, and anxiety hit full-throttle, my natural response was I have to fend for myself. I had a therapist who specialized in childhood sexual abuse tell me that the anxiety was always there, it was just dormant.

*"My mommy had so much happen to her, it was hard for her to see her worth. How could she when most of her adolescent life consisted of*

*men treating her badly. She felt that that's what she was worth. She felt dirty inside. She felt dirty from all the shame these abusers put onto her. None of it was hers. And none of it was her fault.*

*She hit a wall. She was going in circles and could not figure out how to love herself. She tried everything. She would google different ways. She journaled. Yoga really helped her a lot. She was able to connect to herself this way and intimately begin her healing journey. It was not easy for her because she had so much to heal through. But my mommy never gave up. She always kept trying. Even when she couldn't figure it out."*

I would cry in frustration because I could not figure out how to love myself. I ended up mimicking girls I would see in south beach who would stick their chest out, arch their backs and flick their hair from side to side. I had convinced myself that I could be like them and then I would know how to love myself because that is what it looked like to me. But that wasn't me. And by trying to fake it, I wound up broken as I didn't want to feel the pain. But I had no clue how to let it go.

I remember listening to inspirational quotes such as the Japanese proverb "Fall down seven times, stand up eight." While these inspirational words stated helpful in my subconscious, I needed more, and it felt like nothing felt like it helped. I had hit rock bottom. But this is my story, and this is what made me. Even on a subconscious level, this positivity I was bringing in was helping me.

# RECONNECTING WITH A HIGHER-POWER

*"My mommy always loved God. That is her Father. Ever since she came home in the first grade from her Catholic school and found out other families had two parents. She came home that day and asked her mommy why she didn't have a daddy? Her mom's answer was 'you don't have one.' She sat in the bathroom and started talking to God. She said, 'okay God. You are my Father forever."*

Someone suggested that I go back to God. I had completely forgotten about God and my relationship with Him. I had been so busy trying to figure everything out on my own. I hadn't remembered to pray. I wasn't even showing gratitude for the meals I was eating every day. It was so bad that when I ate with other people, my hand would shake so badly with fear that I'd embarrass myself. A prayer of gratitude was the last thing on my mind.

*"My mom was surrounding herself with the wrong kinds of people, including men and in her love life. She was looking for love in all the wrong places because she could not find it from within. She started talking to a megastar, and she'll probably talk more about that later in the book, but although they both gifted each other with priceless gifts in each other's lives, it was hard for her. He wrote 'How to Love' about her and while it precisely spoke of what she was feeling, every time she heard the song, she would cry. It always reminded her of the truth of her past and pain."*

I was really busy spinning around in circles. Knowing that God was always my true Father, and remembering my connection to this Higher-Power had me running back to God. (When I say God in here, I am referring to Jah/Allah/Yahweh/Source/ The Creator of all that is...All the same in my book), It dawned on me that I'd forgotten about my relationship with God, knowing that I viewed Him as my true Father. I then decided to run back to prayer. On the first Sunday after my 26th birthday, I went to church for the first time in years. And while I'm not a huge advocate on church per se, I do think there is something special about congregating in unison to do something spiritual; whatever that may be.

For me, it was my way of learning to be grateful again. I remember asking a friend Becky, "how can I get close to God again?" Her response was "it's like you have to beg God and let Him know that you desire to be closer to Him." So, I began to beg God to help me get close to the Spirit that created mountains and oceans, all then galaxies in the Universe. And it worked! I felt it. I began building a very intimate relationship with Him. I began feeling grateful more often and began to see that all I had gone through was never for no reason. I began to find meaning in my life, knowing that I had a relationship with Source. Life really is what we make it, even if that entails an "imaginary" relationship with the unseen Spirit world.

I had never been into reading the *bible*. I remember being in Catholic school and being forced to read the bible and I just couldn't understand it! But now when I went back to the bible, (along with the Quran and other "Holy" books,) for the first time, I could understand everything! I definitely took what felt right with my soul and left behind anything I didn't agree with or sounded like it was coming from an unloving place since God is Love. I think what happened was, my mind was just open to all things inspirational. All the verses I read during this transformational year of my life pertained to helping me overcome my low self-esteem, due to all of my childhood wounds. One verse that truly helped me, and still helps me to this day is Psalms 139: 13-17: "For You created my inmost being; you knit me together in my mother's womb. I praise You because I am fearfully and wonderfully made; Your works are wonderful. I know that full well." This verse helped me to praise God from the depths of my being because it taught me that He created me and not that I created myself. This particular verse led me to question why I dared to hate myself and my life which He had created. How dare I feel ugly? Based on the shame past predators unrightfully put onto me! After meditating with this verse, I felt like how dare I have the audacity to insult God's creation and perfect expression of who I am and what my essence is by not appreciating me? We come here as a ray of the Universe's co-creation. We are all born for a reason greater than ourselves.

Another verse that helped me value my being is the Genesis 1:27 passage "in the image of God, He created them." This verse taught me that I must be great the way that I am because I am made in the image of God and in His likeness; made of the same stuff He is made of. God is Divine light, then we are Divine light too. God is love, then I am love too. This passage also inspires me to be creative and to create because God/ Source is the Creator, then we are all creators as well.

A verse in Peter 3:5 helped me distinguish outer confidence from true confidence, "your beauty should not come from outward adornment, such as elaborate hairstyles and the wearing of gold jewelry or fine clothes. Rather, it should be that of your inner self, the unfading beauty of a gentle and quiet spirit, which is of great worth in God's sight." When we die, we don't take our bodies with us when we leave as that's going to decay eventually. What does matter is how we choose to live our lives, what were our spirits like? What love did we share with others and how beautiful did we let our souls shine? The inspiration I received from the Bible and from my relationship with Source, helped me understand what true confidence really is.

I am grateful for that hellish year of 25, because without it, I don't think I would have appreciated God as much. (I did also have an energy healer I was seeing around this time that a woman's 25ᵗʰ year is a very challenging one for them.) Once day I cried saying "God, if I had to go through that all over again just to get to this point with You, I would do it countless times." And this is how I feel about all things or events that may seem challenging or even horrible. Deep down our souls know why it chooses to go through certain things, long before even being born into this life. It is all in Divine Order. For this, I am grateful.

From that moment on, I began using tools that really helped me begin to live the life I wanted to create for myself.

# Discovering Yoga

One day while I was working at a bar, one of my coworkers suggested I tried a free yoga class they did every Wednesday evening outdoors by a bay area. He said, I reminded him of the teacher because she was like me in the sense that she was always smiling. Once I tried yoga, I was hooked. My coworker was right about the teacher. She did smile a lot and was very charismatic. But what I fell in love with was much deeper than that. The practice of yoga did something to my soul. It made me feel like I could finally listen to what was going on inside. I felt engaged, challenged, capable, and connected to my inner being.

I understand that different forms of exercises rock different people's boats. Some might really be into spinning classes or weight-lifting. But for me, yoga was really life-changing. It was definitely a key element in restoring me to a healthy state. It was a pillar for me as I began my deep and arduous healing journey. It was fun and it became my happy place. It was the place where I didn't worry, and I could just be with- myself. Not only did I end up feeling more aligned within my body and physique, but I began to lean out and feel strong within my inner being as well as outward. It always makes my spirit feel good. I left every time spent on my yoga mat feeling more alive, more open and more connected to my soul.

Yoga did something even greater for me. It made me become more self-confident. In yoga, it is suggested to always begin with an intention and to breathe that intention into your every movement and into your every breath. You go within and without. You begin praying with your intention into a moving meditation practice on your mat for a sacred amount of time. During your yoga, let's say you forget what your intention was at the beginning of your practice, it's okay because your intention is permeating through your subconscious and all through your cells and is being breathed through your pores.

*"My mommy would start her practice over and over with the intention for more self-confidence. She would get on her mat and start breathing and moving into a sacred prayer. She would move her body with confidence. Her mind was fixated on confidence, and she eventually began believing in this confidence. For her, this was like an exercise that grew her confidence little by little, every practice."*

My thoughts were "I am confident," over and over. I began to exude this confidence through every motion my body was making. I'm not going to sit here and lie and say all I needed for self-confidence was yoga- no. But I will say that yoga was a huge tool in my self-confidence and personal path of healing. I began to view yoga as a prayer with my inner Self.

Yoga and my own meditation practice helped me to become aware of myself. How many people are walking around completely unaware of themselves and of the way they behave towards others? For one to be self-confident, one must be aware of the Self. For you need to be aware of what you are being confident in. With self-awareness, I began to say "Ah, this is who I am. This is who I am not." I began to say positive affirmations and give myself positive self- talk as I was in a meditative state saying things such as "I accept me fully. These are what my values are. This is my voice, and this is my truth." I began to really look at these things with intimacy. I began building a closer relationship with myself through my yoga practice.

There's something magical about becoming self-aware and knowing precisely who you are and what you are. For we are all truly divine essence. We are energy. And since energy can never be created nor destroyed, you can never be destroyed. Once you become aware of yourself, there is no limit to your self-confidence. Self-confidence resides deep within you, and anything that lies within is infinite.

I traveled to India for my 27th birthday and advanced my training as a yoga instructor. This opened me up to so much more. When I went back to Miami, I was like I cannot keep doing the same thing, living this party fast life. I decided to leave my comfort zone and move to L.A. When I first got to L.A. someone told me "Vanessa, L.A. doesn't just have earthquakes. It has human earthquakes too. This city will shake you up so badly, you won't know what happened to you."

Growing up with so much trauma, I became a pro at blocking out any bad experiences. It probably began happening in the bathroom when I was 4 that one night. I had a childhood best friend that would always ask me how I was always able to do that? Well, that was my coping mechanism. In L.A. I faced all that came with trauma. There was no more running away. California was a powerful life lesson for me, spiritually, emotionally, and mentally. It was a time in my life where I had to muster up more inner strength than I thought was humanly impossible. While the pain felt unbearable, it taught me who I really am and what great strength lies within us all. My experience allowed me to meet that strength in a very intimate way. It allowed me to find the warrior within my soul.

*"My mom went to L.A. to have me. She got pregnant with me one year after she moved there. I was supposed to happen- this way. She thought she was moving to L.A. to get focused, but she needed to have me to learn a lot of things. So when she arrived in L.A., she still kept doing the same things as before. Still dating the same kinds of men, not showing herself that she loves herself. She was still hanging out in the party scene and not really taking life seriously."*

Yoga pushes you. Yoga takes you deeper. It allows you to get in touch with your spirit; with your soul. Yoga goes beyond the mind to awareness of breath. Take a moment right now to become aware of your breath. Pause. Feel that? Most people who have practiced yoga have heard the instructor say, "as long as you you're breathing, you're doing it right." Yoga is not so much about doing the poses "right" or pushing yourself hard. It's about honoring your own individual practice and staying aware of your breath, mind, and your energy field. A lot of times, it's simply about witnessing the witness. That's basically what meditation is.

Mind, body, and spirit are always connected. Yoga literally means union; for union of the mind, body, and spirit. It's a practice of alignment. It's a practice of finding balance within yourself. A practice of inner peace- kinetic meditation. It is a practice that can and will draw you closer to yourself. I had a therapist tell me once "self-empowerment and self-love come from self-respect and from self-acceptance." None of this will happen overnight. Rome was not built overnight. And quite frankly, nothing great is built overnight. Now, I'm also not saying that yoga will solve all of this for you, nor is it for everybody; but I will say that yoga will help. Yoga/ meditation will reveal you to yourself.

They say how you do one thing is how you show up to do everything. What you notice in yourself when you're on your mat, you will also notice when you are off your mat. For instance, when I mentioned using the intention of self-confidence on your mat. As you move and breathe through this intention, you will notice its manifestation in other areas of your life. Another example is, you may notice that you show up on your mat every time clenching your jaw, tightening your fists and being full of rigidity. This is a replication of how you are showing up in your everyday life. You may then decide to loosen up a bit in general. You can use this awareness to see what areas of your life need a little bit of tweaking so you can improve yourself.

Evolution is the one constant in the Universe. It is why we are here on the planet. All of life, from the beginning of time, has been evolving. That means there's hope. Lol. No but for real, why the fuck wouldn't I do every single thing in my power to advance that process of self-evolution?

One of my biggest tools along this, what has felt strenuous, journey of mine has been my Higher- Self. The part of ourselves that is intricately connected to our soul. For the soul knows exactly why it is here. It knows exactly what the process of evolution looks like for us on an individual level. No matter what the journey looks like, your soul is always here to evolve. My friend Desi would say it best when she said "I really believe that even when really bad things happen to us, it's for good. No matter what it is. I really do believe that." Your soul knows why it chose to incarnate in this exact life as your exact self. The soul is the all- knowing aspect of ourselves. The part that is less connected with the ego. A mantra I repeat to myself constantly every day is "less ego, more soul." The Higher- Self will always send you signals whether through your gut, signs, or your intuition. The more you honor and listen to yourself, the more present it becomes in your life. This will bring you closer and closer into alignment with your souls higher calling.

None of our past trauma dictates who we are, and yet every trauma makes you who you are. Having not lived your life the exact way it was, you would not be who you are today. And yet you can change at any given moment. What are you willing to become, despite all that you have felt or experienced? In spite of all that the world told you that you are.

*"My mom has overcome a lot of profound trauma. Way more than the average. She has come a long way on her journey, and she still has a ways to go. Her spirit is what has kept her going. It's that little voice inside that has always been telling her to keep on going and to keep on smiling. Through that voice she has found a spark of hope and faith and that's all you need."*

From the day I was born, I never gave up. I've always been the ambitious type. And I'm not going to quit, nope I'm not going to do it. I will always strive to grow and be the best I can be. We came here for reasons beyond our comprehension. Our souls signed up for this. It's only right to honor that and be 100% true to ourselves. I want to reach my full potential and tap into the true desires of my unique soul. And so can you. I don't believe that anyone was born to quit or sell themselves short. You owe it to yourselves to overcome your biggest life lessons and any challenges or fears. It is seriously for the evolution of your soul. Step your game up, level up, and fight the good fight till the end & make sure to enjoy the ride- it's all we've got.

## CHAPTER 1

# Don't Worry, Be Happy

When things get rough, you already know, that it's time to get tough! You know that it's time to fight through. And you know that at one time or another, life is going to hit you with a banger and it's going to feel like it's really hard to fight back. The good news is there is always hope. If you are still alive, there is always hope. Ever since I was little, I would try to find ways to be happy. Even if it's just to look for the sunshine. Even if the sun isn't shining outside. I would focus on anything that would make me even think of the thought of happiness because everything else seemed better than the pain.

At the time, I didn't **real-eyes** that what I was doing was suppressing my emotions. Nevertheless, the coping mechanism I chose at 12 allowed me to develop a strong muscle for positive thinking. I would just keep looking for better things to focus on. When things were crazy at home, I would want to run away to a cave somewhere. I used to hide in my room and convince myself that things were not as bad as they actually were. On one side of the spectrum, what I was actually doing was cultivating hope and dreaming of life actually being something beautiful. Why drill hateful thoughts in your head 24/7? Perspective is always a choice.

Let's say you are in the middle of chaos, and you decide you know what, life is not that bad and it could always be worse... can you find some truth in this knowing? At what point is your reality actually good or bad? And contingent upon who or what premises? Your reality is always exactly what you perceive it to be.

My friend and her brother grew up in the same household with a very abusive father. He used to punish them for small things and would lock them in a dark closet for hours at a time. She found a small rug in the closet and would pretend it was for the use of a magic carpet ride where she was able to go anywhere in the world. She made a terrifying experience into a fun one full of magical possibilities. Today she is a talented singer/songwriter who uses her imagination as a tool that helps her. Yet her brother on the other hand, used to be locked up in the same closet, would use his time getting very angry the whole time. And till this day he harbors his anger a lot and finds himself getting in tiffs where he's been arrested on certain occasions due to the amount of anger he carries within himself. Her brother never channeled his anger for the better nor did he use his perspective to view the time spent in the closet as an opportunity for a magic carpet ride.

That's all life is – perspective. Ah, the freedom to choose your perspective in any given moment and situation. Perception can determine whether you have a good day or a bad one. Every day you are given a full 24 hours to do whatever it is that you want to do. And whether you enjoy your day or not, depends on more than outside factors. The choice is yours to worry about a situation, or enjoy your day, be grateful, and serve others. You can choose to allow yourself to be devastated or great. You have the choice to combat any negative thought. You have the choice to be great. You have the choice to heal. It blows my mind how vast our world is with 8 billion people and not one person has the answer to all. This is very liberating to know that this means no one is better than you. No one is perfect. No one has it all figured out. There is a freedom here with this knowing. We are free. Free to think, free to choose. We are even free to invent something new, who's to say it wouldn't be the world's next greatest invention? Because we are free to perceive things as we wish, we have access to choose whatever we want to think within our given birthright.

The key is to focus on your beliefs and how you want to reshape them and cultivate them. This is how creativity happens. Oftentimes, we center into a part of our soul that allows us space and room to tap into higher levels of our true selves. Our Higher-Self ALWAYS leads us in the right direction. So, if you're constantly following the true yet subtle voice of your soul, you will be able to eventually think positive and live a life more in alignment with love. Love is the essence of who and what we truly are. It is our

Higher-Self. It is what babies are comprised of. I had my Kamden and knew in those few months with him that he was beaming with a frequency unlike adults for sure. He was pure love. Sometimes I wish adults were more like their childlike selves because they have a high ethereal intelligence and sense of purity. Through living from a place of love, one lives with virtues of a higher frequency. When one is living from a place of love, from the place of their soul, it becomes easy to live in joy, humility, peace, harmony, and all things positive. When one lives from this higher center of self within them, they will always be guided towards the way of the light, no matter how dark things may get. When one lives from this place it becomes easy to listen to Self.

However, most people tend to follow the perceptions of others, never taking the time to question what they themselves believe. It is easy to get distracted and influenced by external stimuli which leads us away from our soul. The more grounded you are in your soul, the more confidently you can take on every given moment.

Let's say you're out on a glorious Saturday afternoon having chai tea lattes with friends and all of a sudden someone says, "ugh I hate how it smells in here." Now the vibe is off for all of you, even if you don't smell anything bad. Energy transfers. So most likely, you or the whole group has a new perspective and are in a negative mood. Depending on the individual perspective, and how a person processes the present moment, the rest of the day can go down a spiral. When this happens to me, I remind myself that I am here now in the present moment. Each present moment has within it a gift, the presence of the present. This is why the present moment is called a present. There is an ever-present aliveness that is born in every new moment allowing for pure potentiality to take any variation of course that is chosen. It all depends on perception... There is always a choice in every given present moment.

I constantly work on my emotional intelligence and decide for myself that I am not going to let one moment, or several moments, mess up the rest of my day. We are all alive at the same time seeing with different lenses. Babies come into this world with so much happiness and a natural state of just being? Sometimes to the point of bliss! They're usually smiling and when they cry, they can easily change their smile to laughter if something fun gets their attention. It's as if they never really had any true problems to begin with.

The truth is most problems can be resolved. And for the ones that can't be solved, life will go on anyways. So how you perceive the situation from there is always up to you. Most people stay stuck, clinging to a problem, person or event that hurt them. Someone can do the smallest thing, without even knowing at times, and this problem ruins our mood for the entirety of the day. For some people, this becomes their way of life. Are you going to keep holding on or become fluid with life and move on with it?

The motivational speaker Zig Ziggler said "A negative thinker finds difficulty in every opportunity. A positive thinker finds opportunity in every difficulty." To reprogram your mind to a positive perspective, practice focusing on the many possible solutions to any problem. And if you can't change the situation, you can always choose to accept it. This is always a possible solution. There are always multiple options to how you are going to view the hand you were dealt. No matter what this hand is.

There is no point in fighting and wrestling with life by not accepting what is. That is the perfect recipe for you to be unhappy. Acceptance is to not fight against what is. It is to allow a situation to be exactly as it is. It is fully embodying the very real phrase of: "it is what it is."

It's really easy to get caught up in the idea that we have all the control in the world. This sense of control gives us a false sense of security and power. The truth is we only have so much control. Ever talk to someone who has had a near death experience? One of the first things that person will say is "I realized I had no control." For some reason, we are convinced we can control every aspect of our lives, and therefore must be responsible for everything that happens to us. So much to the point that we at times feel guilty for things occurring that had nothing to do with us and were far from our control.

We try and try to figure out how to control every situation, every single second, instead of going with the flow, feeling the breeze, slowing down and taking in the clear blue sky. We take this life so seriously yet knowing that this is all temporary as we are all immortal. This is but a glimpse in the totality of our true infinite existence.

What if problems weren't even real? Growing up I used to hear my family worrying about some of the dumbest things. "What would Aunt Suzette say about xyz? Why isn't the microwave working? What will they think?" I used to tell them that their problems weren't even really big problems when people are out in the world starving and have real problems. They would pause or a second and give that some thought, but they were in the habit of simply finding things to worry about unnecessarily. In reality, a few months from now, today's problems won't even be an issue.

By all means, do your best to make the best out of every situation as stress can literally kill you. When you start to notice that your life is filled with worry and you are waking up with anxiety, use that as an indicator that it's time to take a step back and put things back into perspective.

Stress will age you. I noticed within myself, the times I have looked the youngest are times I spent an ample amount of time smiling and living carefree. I have a friend who is aging gloriously, and I think it is contributed to her carefree perspective in life. Her name is NikkiMak and I'll never forget what she once told me, "Vanessa, I never stress because whatever is going to happen is going to happen anyway. There's no point in stressing." She is right. It is what it is. What will be will be. The next time you are stressed over a problem you have no control over, ask yourself if it's even worth stressing over. If not, why bother? Life is so short you might as well at least try living with no worries. Do you think God wants to see you unhappy? God doesn't want you to be stressed. The Creator did not create you to live a life full of worry.

A bible verse I love as a reminder is Matthew 6: 25-27:

*"Therefore I tell you, do not worry about your life, what you will eat or drink; or about your body, what you will wear. Is not life more than food and the body more than clothes? Look at the birds of the air; they do not sow or reap or store away in marks, and yet your heavenly Father feeds them. Are you not much more valuable than they? Can any one of you by worrying add a single hour to your life."*

If animals live their lives with no worries, then why wouldn't we (the species with the highest level of intelligence) humans live that way too? No one gains a thing from worrying. So often when we do worry, there's no real reason to. So often we worry about not having this or that, or what could go wrong when the future hasn't even happened yet.

I have wasted so much time worrying about unnecessary things such as when my career would take off. And then I **real-eyes-ed** that what I was wanting couldn't possibly come right at this second; and worrying wasn't going to speed any of it up in reality.

This **real-eyes-ation** brought me to understand:

- To reside in the present moment. Even if I have to keep coming back to it over and over.
- To slow down and relish in the joy that life is a journey.
- That as long as I'm working towards my career goals, they will one day be attained.
- Focusing on worrying about things of the past or the future are not in alignment with nature.

Sure, you can use it for reference when needed, but when you get to the point of worrying and it has no benefit to what's going on right now, then it becomes irrational behavior.

I once had a therapist tell me if I kept worrying about a bad past experience, I'd be living from a place of fear, which keeps you away from the present moment. Same thing goes for worrying about what's already destined to happen to you. If you're destined for something, beyond your control, why keep worrying about it? There's no point. Try living in the present moment so you're not living in the lens of what was or what will be. She said you will always be at odds with what will be; again, taking you out of the present moment and causing you to live in fear- False Evidence Appearing Real. Fear is an illusion. So is worrying.

Living in a constant state of fear is asking for yourself to live a miserable life. Living in a constant state of anxiety and worry is ultimately setting yourself up for defeat; without giving yourself the opportunity to live from the opposite of fear- love. Rather, choose to go about your day with an essence of love. Spread love; to yourself and to everyone you encounter. What you're giving out- you are getting right back to yourself because we are all mirrors for each other- reflecting ourselves to each other. Walking in love and not fear is really choosing not to worry on a moment-by-moment basis and choosing love. It is really about attuning to love in the present moment. Even when it's the last thing you feel like feeling. That's usually an indicator that love needs to be called in.

Having deep reverence for the lessons that come your way, and love for your soul in the process of it all, is the hard part.. Compassion. This becomes easier to do through mindfully slowing down and coming to the place within your center where you can see things for what they are. Where you can do so lovingly. Just through having the intention to do this, you will begin to cultivate this practice of reverence.

When in reality, what is- is what is. Acceptance is a healer. When you can learn to accept really the entirety of your life as a whole; there are aspects of your human experience that automatically become healed.

Accepting life is about pausing and looking at all the beauty around you in any given moment. Accepting that you may not have what you want right now but understanding that you may still get it at a later time leaves room for hope. For anything is possible, so leave room for limitless possibilities to occur. Learn to accept the possibility that things may not pan out the way you want them and that's okay too. Life is interesting.

Life is always happening... it never stops. We might as well make every moment as sweet as possible. No matter how challenging that may be.

(Sometimes, it's not that you don't believe in yourself, it's that you can't believe that you do believe in yourself).

# DEALING WITH WORRY AND SADNESS

Growing up, when I was sad, I exercised a muscle for developing a positive perspective. I did this by taking note of how much I hated my sadness. I would search for things to make me happy. I used to look out the window at the beautiful sunset or the pink and purple clouds in the sky. I found joy in the beauty around me. Even if it was raining outside, I could choose to look at the beauty of the contrast of the colors emanating within nature. Such as the bright greens in the trees against the dark midnight blue thunder storming sky. I always searched for an escape, a getaway, something to ease the pain.

It's healthy to face whatever is bothering you. If you suppress the pain, suppression turns into repression which then leads to depression. All energy needs to move through you so that it can be released. Especially the heavier emotions such as sadness. It's important to choose to feel the pain for a time, then let it go and look to the light. It's important to keep feeling your feelings fully as they come and go (as they surely always will,) so that they can transcend. You'll notice you and your life becomes lighter too. Just your everyday has more of an ease to it once you're no longer holding onto what no longer is serving you. I'll speak about this more in chapter 10. The next time you find yourself worried or upset or sad, **real-eyes** that you have a choice of what kind of perspective you want to have, a choice of how you wish to view things including the things that make you sad. It is important to honor your feelings, but it is also to know that you have the capacity to have emotional intelligence. With emotional intelligence, one is better able to be grounded in their emotions and one is more in control of how they will choose to react.

Most of us get worried then try to forget about it all. We consume ourselves with TV, food, alcohol, drugs, shopping, sex addictions, etc., just as a form of a distraction. The next time you're worried or sad about something, think about what worries you. Ask yourself "will this kill me?" Ask yourself seriously, "what's the worst that can happen?" Then **real-eyes** that it hasn't gotten to the worst yet and it may never get that bad.

*"My mommy went through one of the hardest things for a human to experience- she lost a child. It doesn't matter if I was a 9-month-old baby. It is still very hard to go through. No one really gets anything they cannot handle. I knew that my mom would be able to handle going through something like this. Everything in her life prepared her to be able to handle this. I never want her to worry about losing me in this realm, because I am always here with her. She has no need to worry. There are so many positive things that came from this experience. Things she is not even aware of yet. It was a blessing in disguise. It's always good to look for the blessing in every curse."*

I also recommend that no matter how bad things may get, **real-eyes** that no matter how bad the situation, it could always be worse. Always! And you will be okay. If you are alive, there is some part of you that is doing okay- clearly. It's like the Bob Marley song Three Little Birds where he says "don't worry, about a thing- cause every little thing is gonna be alright." There is profound truth in this **real-eyes-ation.** I'm not suggesting ignoring everything that's going on in your life that doesn't feel good. But prioritize and take hold of your perspective on things. With this knowing, I do encourage you to look for beauty around you. Look for beauty within you. I encourage you to find things that will make your soul smile. When applying a positive attitude to your life, this will help you manage your emotions in a mature manner. It will also help with your overall emotional intelligence on a personal and interpersonal level. Focusing on positivity, will help you improve the overall quality of your life. This will change your focus for the better. Your soul will begin to resonate with positivity and attract positive energy.

# MAKTUB - IT IS WRITTEN

From a very young age, **I real-eyes-ed** that everything happens for a reason. At least there is a lesson in everything that occurs. I personally don't believe in regrets because I believe at some point or another, one wanted to do whatever they chose to do. And however bad the incident may have been, it has shaped you to be who you are at this very moment. All of our experiences shape us into who we are now and who we will later become. There is some reason for why things happen the way that they do. Sometimes, it is solely to learn a lesson. Whether you catch it or not is always up to you. This is why I love taking time to reflect. There is usually a lot to gain from deep reflection. When I discovered a very envious "best friend," had hexed me with black magic, I had myself tattooed with the word *"Maktub,"* which means "it is written" in Arabic. (Interestingly enough a couple of years later, at 27 years old, I discovered my father was half Lebanese and the Arabic language is a part of my bloodline.)

The day after I found out about her curse, my mother ended up in a strange car accident. Four people were involved in her car yet she was the only one who was hurt. And she was hurt bad. She had 6 broken ribs and bleeding in her brain. She spent 3 months in the Intensive Care Unit. What made this experience even more painful was the bleeding in her brain caused her to act different.

Her mannerisms were different. Her eyes wandered. After I learned about the curse, my life changed. I knew I could choose how to perceive situations. I remember looking for signs of strength and hope everywhere. There was a song by Kanye West that said, "what doesn't kill me makes me stronger," and I used this to hype up my faith and believe that things would turn for the better. Thankfully my mother had a lot of support from loved ones and people who would bring her food and pray for her. By the grace of God, within a few months my mom was healed.

While the passing of my son Kamden was, in medical terms, due to Zellweger's syndrome... he also passed away as a result of black magic. A black pigeon hit the exact center of my living room window the day before my scheduled cesarean. Because my family is from Haiti, they knew right away when they saw the blood from the pigeon that this was a result of sorcery. While I know this to be true, I also knew that this is what the Lord the Creator ordained because it wouldn't have happened if it wasn't in God's plan as well. I'm too holy and way too connected to God for this to have been all of the devil's plan. And when I say devil, I am referring to intense dark energy.

Sure, I believe black magic exists, but I do not believe in its power over me. Not when we have an Almighty Creator who is the the true power source! The power of black magic, the workings man thinks he can do with man, cannot compete with the power of the Creator. When I became aware of all of this black magic, I chose to use this as an opportunity to increase my faith. I chose to believe that, regardless of how difficult it really was, it was happening for my higher good, to make me stronger and to teach me the important lesson that some people really do have cruel intentions and evil hearts. While I believe in justice wholeheartedly, I also believe in karma. I think there is something so beautiful about trusting Life/ The Universe/ God/ Karma because things will always have to go back to balance as is the natural accord of evolution. Things are always brought back into balance. People might as well live in trust. With trust there is an ease of worry.

When I chose to get the word "Maktub," tattooed on me, it was a reclamation of my trust in what God's plan was for my life. I believe that certain things happen for certain reasons to elevate our souls and to shape us in specific ways that are critical to our own individual journey. Whether these things are "good," or "bad," there is something greater than us co-creating things at some level for our highest good. It is Maktub when one takes an extra 30 minutes than planned to rest and on their way home, they see an accident that could have been they could have been a part of had they not taken the nap. Maktub is like my story with my precious Kamden. It was written. The Creator allowed this to happen, and I am only compelled to believe that Kamden and I agreed to a contract to experience this monumental yet shape-shifting tragedy prior to either of us entering this world. It was too transformational. It was too intense. Not to mention, when I was pregnant, I lived with a roommate who was also pregnant by another basketball player at the same time as me. Both of our partners at the time would compete against each other's teams. She and I were both having boys. And her baby boy was perfectly fine. It was a specific situation- something like my Kamden being born with a fatal disease and a zero chance of surviving was a part of our destinies.. It was already written. Too many things happen to individuals that is way too specific to them and their path beyond our understanding- *Maktub*.

# WHAT THIS BELIEF HELPED ME REAL-EYES:

1.  I can be content because there is a greater reason why things are happening in my life, whether I agree with them or not. And right now, I am okay. Heck it already happened. It's called life. Thank goodness it's not worse.

2.  If everything happens for a reason, then it must be for a good reason on some accord. The choice to look at things good or bad is always yours. No one is hanging anything over your head saying you have to look at things negatively. No one is saying that you have to worry, except for most likely you. No one is dictating how one should live their life and that be the only right way.. This world is full of possibilities in how you choose to perceive your reality. And who is to say it is wrong? Why not get creative and come up with a new way to perceive things that are more in alignment with a stress-free attitude. The sayings "good vibes only," and "peace and love," can be your everyday truth. It's all about how you choose to see things.

# Don't Compare Yourself to Others:

Care about others, have compassion for them but don't compare yourself to them. Each of us walk on our own path. We may help each other out along the way and walk with each other to get where we are going, but in all actuality, this is your journey and no one else's. Don't place yourself above or below others for any reason. Learn to be secure within your being for the unique person that you are. The sacred life within you and around you is your very own and no one can take that away from you.

It can be difficult to live in a society that does not encourage a healthy self-esteem. I studied with an amazing Indian Guru named Anand Mehrotra, who talked about how fucked up America can be. In America specifically, from early childhood, parents teach their kids how to be competitive. They'll gloat about how their child won first place in this and how their daughter is the best at that... We are taught at a very early age to compare, compete, and feel less than or better than someone else yet we did not come here to live in comparison to others and I don't believe that attitude is healthy or even rational.

How ignorant and irrational is it for me to compare myself to Sarah and be jealous that she has more Instagram likes than I do or has a nicer car than mine? Each soul, each life is here on their own track with their own gains and losses. None of what goes on in anyone's life has anything to do with you unless they willingly include you into their life and that is usually to stand in from an objective lens. It is never personal so why do you get into it? How does someone's gain make them a better person than you are? What's yours is yours and what's mine is mine and vice versa. So there is no need to ever worry about what is for someone else. Again, it has nothing to do with you. If it's not inspiring you, don't hate on it. The least you can do is not worry about it at all.

Not to mention the self-sabotage that occurs when one does this. We hurt ourselves when we begin to compare, compete and be jealous of others. This always stems from a deep sense of insecurity within one's being. When one lets their insecurities fester within them, not only does it grow but it can become toxic if you don't tend to it and handle it. Your aura and your energy become off.

*"My mom struggled with this a lot after I transitioned. She was feeling so many icky feelings within her that made her act in ways out of her character. She became plagued by the spirit of jealousy and envy."*

I definitely saw how ugly the green-eyed monster can be in others, specifically in the ex-best friend who I mentioned earlier and a few other conflicted souls I have come across over the years. But I say this to say that I also found it within myself, later in life, but nevertheless I experienced it. And this is nothing I am proud to admit, however it is good to see what it is that you do not ever want to be. I **real-eyes** that so much of the green-eyed monster is correlated to a person's deep insecurities and pain. And it has nothing to do with the other person and it has everything to do with you. I felt it when life hit me rock bottom. I felt it when I was not happy with myself nor with my life. I am honestly happy I had my own phase of such darkness within my being so I can understand what all of it is. I am human and I think it is important for every human to feel every single thing possible to see what we want to be like and what we don't want to be like. And to know that these emotions are okay. Being human can be complicated. I think it is important to focus on trying to be the very best version of yourself as a means of living in your highest light... living in your highest truth.

There is beauty in your own journey, how can you honor it if you're so preoccupied with what others have and how they think, what they have or what you don't have. Look, everybody's got something. I've always had this strong belief that we are all equals. Why? Because we are all made of the same stuff. We all came from the same place, and we all go the same way. We all bleed, shit, cry, suffer, have feelings, and we are all going to die. What one person chooses to do with their life doesn't make them better than anyone else. Now, everyone has free will. That is between you and you. It has nothing to do with anyone else... So long as you're not hurting others.

Comparing yourself is a form of self-hatred. If you love yourself enough, you won't need to compare yourself to anyone else because you are whole and fulfilled. *"My mommy felt a lot of the comparison before she came to full terms of healing with her father abandoning her. She believed she was so unworthy at the root of her soul and that was false. So she struggled until she could forgive the man that abandoned her from birth."* Comparing yourself to others can be destructive to your self-esteem. It can be irrational. It's one thing to compare two identical things, but no two humans are exactly the same. You can have no clue where someone else is in their life journey. I know a woman who wanted to write songs. She got opportunities to participate in sessions with Grammy award-winning artists. But her attitude was negative, and her soul was punctured, because she kept comparing herself to others in the studio. "They already have Grammy's. They already have mansions; success." Sure, they were successful but they put in the work and they too had to start at A and then B before they got to Z. She could have used that as inspiration and as a great opportunity to learn from greats. But instead, she was upset because she was working for free, as they had done once upon a time. She wasn't there yet.

Each life journey is unique. Look at the greats. Look at them for inspiration, not to bring yourself down. Study the success of others and the paths they have chosen, so that you can learn how to make similarly positive choices. The truth is, no one is better or worse than anyone else. Some people may not want to believe that because it does something for their ego. But it's true. We are all human beings. Look at chickens for instance, a whole coop is just filled with chickens. Sure, one may take on this role as the head honcho, but in reality, they are all just chickens and that is just primal bullshit. There is nothing enlightening about comparison just to get a false sense of gratification to stroke your ego. I will go into this further in a later chapter. But it's real. No need to worry about things that are irrational to begin with.

When someone tries to compete with me, I don't worry because I know it's only in their minds, therefore they already lost. It's an imaginary race that only they are a part of on their own accord in their own imagination. They'd rather go out of their way to create a false competition. It's like, who's competing? And it's like, they're so focused on me when there's better things to focus on. I know I am going to spend my time focusing on my journey, where I want to go and what I am going to do to get there. I don't have time to waste focusing on others... It's like they say, be busy minding your own business.

# GIVE YOURSELF THE BEST LIFE POSSIBLE:

It is important to give yourself the best life possible. And that includes the best inner world within you. We're so used to living as if everything is outside and we constantly search outside of ourselves; when life is really happening inside of us. For example, you may see people succeeding, doing what may appear to be "better," than you are and yet you have no idea what they did to get there or what their life really looks like. All that focusing on someone else does is steal your joy anyway. You are always in control of what you choose to focus on and how you perceive things. The choice is always there. You can cause yourself more worry or choose not to. You can worry about the big zit on your forehead, or you can choose to appreciate other features you have that make you feel unique and beautiful. This goes for everything.

Find out what's meaningful for you and live your truth out loud. You will never get bored. It's definitely something I am still discovering more and more every day. It's something you don't have to stop discovering. Every new day is a new way to rediscover who you are. Try new things. Try everything. Might as well do what you love because our time is so short here. Why waste your time doing what you don't love just to fail? Just to worry and be even more unhappy? Life is way too short. Just focus on what does make you happy. Spend your time doing what makes you happy. I have a friend that goes by the name of Hocus and he was sharing a beautiful DMT experience with me where he was stating that he had never felt so much love in his life. It was a message from Spirit to not worry. Just live and don't worry. Slow down and do the things that bring you peace. Take baths, go to the spa, get a massage, go for a walk. Give yourself time to rest. Do things that will make you live a stress-free life. This makes total sense when you really think about it.

*"After I left, I just wanted mommy to be happy and to not worry about anything. When her time there is finished, she will be with me again. For now, just be happy and don't worry about anything. There is nothing to worry about. You're still there, so why worry? People are in one dimension and when you die you go to another dimension. You never really die. So why worry?"*

Think about how you spend your everyday and what your thoughts consist of. Are you busy wasting your time thinking about your past or caught up in the future? The Power of Now by Eckhart Tolle is a great tool to be present. I recall reading his book and using practices he suggests such as feeling your hands on the wheel as you are driving to bring your attention back to the present moment. I like to listen to sounds around me, such as the sound of the wind as it is blowing. It is alive and is a good reminder that we are all in the present moment only. It is a waste of time to live ahead in the future or in the past. You can only make change happen in the here and now anyway. You can only be truly alive in the here and now. So, choose to live in the now as much as possible.

This way you won't waste your time focusing on unnecessary things. You don't want your life to pass you on by to feel like it was all a waste. Make it count, every moment. Make the choice to not worry and be happy. You have the power to choose to enjoy your life at the present given moment of your life. You have the power to choose to be happy, every new moment is an opportunity for you to choose, to choose how YOU want to live YOUR life. That has nothing to do with anybody else. You can choose how you perceive thing... How you embrace the moment, and how you view your past. You can choose what to value in life, what to be grateful for.

# Practices/Affirmations to Help You Don't Worry

*Smile more.*

*"I am safe right now."*

*"All is well and wonderful (full of wonder.)"*

*"I do not worry about what others think of me."*

*Exude love in every new moment instead of fear, hatred or worry.*

*Focus on the good things in your life.*

*Create solutions for the things that are not going well.*

*Practice not comparing yourself to others.*

*Understand everyone is on their unique journey and you are on yours.*

*Choose trust instead of worry. They both cannot coexist. The choice of perception is in your power.*

## CHAPTER 2

# Give Thanks and Praises

Marianne Williamson, along with many old-time gurus, say that there are only two emotions: fear and love. Every other emotion stems from one of these. They cannot coexist. Positive emotions emanate from love and negative emotions emanate from fear. Emotions lead to positive or negative behavior. It sucks that, as a culture, we have become so accustomed to speaking badly about others, putting others down to gain a false sense of gratification... To gain a false sense of entitlement. We are so caught up in treating others badly rather than treating people kindly. We need a new culture. One that is of love and exudes loving emotions and behaviors. The truth is, so many people are walking around carrying loads of pain. They're carrying more hurt than they can contain, so it overflows onto others around them. When we learn to have an attitude that gives thanks and praises, we treat ourselves and others with kindness. Those within our community feel better when we treat them with love and the world becomes a better place. We are the only species on Earth that kills its own kind. I don't believe this is natural and definitely not the best way to live our lives. If people appreciated others more, we would acknowledge that each of us serves a special purpose in each other's lives. It's really a gift. Yet so many people are consumed with fear. Have you ever heard someone say how much they just hate everyone? I mean, maybe you've said it a time or two. But let's be real; living like that won't make you happier, nor is it in alignment with your soul. Take note of how often you go to an ugly place in your mind-complaining, criticizing, whining and self-doubting.

How many times do we go through the day cursing, sighing, grunting? How many times do you tense up throughout the day and don't even **real-eyes** it? How often are you not aware of your foot twitching because of anxiety? It's crazy how we live in a society where the negativity is all that is shown on the news. You would think the news we would want to hear consists of more positivity rather than negativity. The news might as well be called negative TV since it's all they show most of the time which honestly leads to so much fear. Watching the news can seriously change your whole demeanor, thought processes and mood. It can keep you in a state of fear. Yet, fear is something that is learned. Scientists have proven that when a baby is born, they come into this world with only two fears- these two fears are incorporated in our DNA as a survival mechanism: the fear of falling, and the fear of loud sounds. Yet it's as if we get older and we become more and more afraid of countless things that are most of the time not rational.

You probably heard the acronym for fear: False Evidence Appearing Real. When you really ask yourself why you are afraid, the answer is usually fictitious. Sometimes it's based on past experiences that may have been traumatic. However, if you are being loving towards yourself, loyal, and respectful, then you will inevitably be that way towards others and you will attract the same from others. Practice getting in the habit of 1. looking at your fears head on. 2. asking yourself whether your fears are even logical. 3. practice being bold enough to get passed those fears by doing exactly what you are afraid of. Fear is such a negative, low vibration to operate in and it is a domino effect. For example, let's say you like a girl and but then you start wondering what people will think, so now your nerves go bad. You become afraid of rejection. Your thoughts go down a spiral where you begin wondering "what will she want with me anyway?" Then you have an influx of unpleasant emotions such as sadness, anger, insecurity. And you end up not doing what you wanted to do all along. You get my drift, negativity attracts negativity.

Let go and surrender all the negative energy, thoughts, actions, and feelings so that the mind is only consumed with joy. Execute fear, get your mind right and follow a new mental pathway. Instead of having these negative thoughts and emotions, practice gratitude and having positive thoughts since this is what controls your behavior. It recently dawned on me that my life could be so much worse! Shit, when I think about it, it's pretty darn wonderful (full of wonder.) The other day, I accidentally hit my head and it hurt really bad. But was I bleeding? No. Was there internal bleeding? I doubt it. But this made me **real-eyes** that it could always be worse- no matter what. As Americans, we take so much for granted. Sometimes, it's good to see how third-world countries are living with little to nothing yet they have joy and gratitude. We could learn a thing or two from them. How often do we stop and think to ourselves, "oh my God, I have all of my limbs and they are functioning well. Thank You so much for my health. Thank you for my family. Thank you for my friends turned into family." The truth is, some of us don't have legs, some of us are living in suffering conditions and aching. There is always something you can find to be grateful for. There are always things you can find to give the Most High thanks and praises. Praises for who you are as a unique being. Thanks and praises that you are growing and evolving as a being. How often do you say "thank you God for keeping me safe at all times. Thank you, Universe, for letting that relationship end because it was toxic for my soul."

I began to **real-eyes** that we are spoiled. We are so comfortable that we tend to forget how fortunate we are as a civilization. What if we didn't evolve to the level that we have? We are intelligent beings, full of limitless potential, each wise in our own way. We are blessed to be in a world with other people. Can you imagine living on Earth all by yourself? We have a voice and the language to express our opinions and feelings. We have a beautiful sun that comes out every single day to shine on us. We have healthy and tasty foods to enjoy! We have the arts and entertainment where you can spend your time in beauty and joy. Can you imagine what your life would be like without music? Without all the things you love? We have something called passion. Everyone is passionate about something. Think about what you enjoy spending your time doing most and that is what you are passionate about.

Love is all around us and within us. So is the Universe/God/ The Most High for Source is love and love resides within you. You are real. You exist! You have yourself! Here you are, right here, right now- always. You were born into this Earth with yourself on your birthday. And you were with yourself before that. You will leave this Earth with yourself. You lie down every single night and wake up every day with yourself. Every single thought is yours, so is every single experience you have. Everything you see, you see with your eyes alone. Everything you hear, you hear with your ears alone. For everything happens within yourself. Where are you witnessing things from? Everything you are perceiving is within yourself. Learn to pay attention to yourself. I'm not talking about being self-absorbed, but about **real-eyes-ing** that you are very, very, precious at the depths of your soul. And you came here to experience yourself in your fullest expression. You are alive right now. You are breathing right now, inhabiting a body that is yours. It's something that only you can feel. It's something that can only be true for you. *My mom is still learning to keep appreciating* *herself. It's a never-ending process.*

# CHERISH YOUR TRUE SELF

The first and most important thing we all ought to cherish is ourselves. When you discover a true gratitude for yourself, you will find love. Through that love you find for self, you will find love for others. How well you treat yourself is reflected in the way you treat others. If you are hateful towards others, you are definitely hateful to yourself; if not more. Same goes for disrespect, ungratefulness, and so on. The way you feel about yourself determines what you attract into your life. If you are critical with yourself, or emotionally abusive, you very well may attract the same type of person in your life. However, if you are being loving towards yourself, loyal, respectful, then you will inevitably be that way towards others and you will attract the same from others.

Too often in our society, people have a dog-eat-dog mentality to try to stay on top with a selfish attitude all because of a false sense of security to be "on top." People completely forget to love themselves and others. Just take a look at people in the grocery store. Look at how people treat customers. Where is the compassion? Where is the gratitude for the precious moment to share love with a complete stranger? Shit, where is the authenticity? Nobody has it figured out so I can't understand why people treat each other so shitty. We're all here trying to do what we came here to do. Why in the world would you not want to live your life in appreciation for yourself and others? A.k.a. love?

A line in a song by Drake goes "Man, I love myself cause I swear that life is just not as fun." Why would a life of self-hatred be more fun than a life of self-love? Should we buy into hate since we were not taught how to love? Since we were not taught how to love ourselves? You would think that that would be the first thing we would to be learning in school and at home. It's just commons sense. Yet this is not the case. Mostly because we come from parents and systems who don't love themselves. I have dealt with self-hatred throughout my entire life. Let's say I take a picture of myself and post it on Instagram or Facebook, or whatever, and I only get a few likes. I may then go so hard on myself and criticize everything about myself, just nitpicking. We are our own biggest critics. But it's time to be our own biggest fans! I can look at the same picture and instead of critiquing everything I think is wrong with me, I can instead focus on every single thing I like. Like, why not? The choice is ours right? And it's our life! If you're tired of feeling terrible about yourself, fuck it! Do the exact opposite and promise yourself you will focus on the positives about yourself and make it a habit. Every day. Promise yourself you will practice giving thanks for who you are as a whole- as a soul.

# Lessons in Self-Love and Gratitude

Look at yourself fully naked in a full-length mirror. Take this as a moment to cherish you and the vessel that you are inhabiting for this lifetime. Instead of doing what you're so used to doing, focusing on all the things you do not like about your body, focus on all the things you do like. You might find it difficult at first, but who are we to not love and appreciate ourselves? The way we view and treat our bodies is a reflection of how we treat ourselves in general. The views we have about ourselves are reflected in the way we treat others and in the way others treat us. If you think you are shit and a nobody, don't be surprised if that's how the world begins to treat you. Whereas, when you begin to think of yourself highly and in a sense of royalty, in a sense of righteousness, the world will reflect those feelings by showing you respect. So, get in front of a mirror. Notice body parts you like, stand in different poses you think look good. Get up close and personal. Many people dissociate from themselves and their bodies...get to know yours. Embrace your beauty, your physique, your curves, muscles, your skin tone, your signature body shape, which only you have and choose to love! Love it all! Love all the good things about yourself, focus on those very things, and feel confident about it. Do this with your face as well. Take notice of your eyes, your cheeks, your jaw line, the curvature of your lips, and your nose. Examine your face- when you smile and when you don't smile. Just focus on the good. **Real-eyes** there is no other person in the world that looks exactly like you. **Real-eyes** the majesty of the Divine Creator and how the Universe was able to create so many unique faces by merging two humans together in love. It is the purest form of art. Give praise for the masterpiece God created as your unique self. Ask yourself what makes you look unique. That, my friend, is what makes you look beautiful.

I always wanted to feel like a queen, so I recently ordered an Isis costume. The Egyptian goddess Isis has always resonated with me. When I first put the costume on, I saw myself in a whole different light. As though I were my own Pharaoh. I took photos of myself in her costume and felt like a multi-raced modern-day Cleopatra. This practice was so healing. I cannot even describe what this has done to my self-image. I was thankful to finally see myself the way I always wanted to envision myself- as a queen. how you view yourself influences the way others see you. How you see yourself in fluences the way others see you. If you feel like a Pharaoh, you'll begin to emanate that energy and it will begin to resonate with others. You always have full control of the way you perceive yourself at any given moment. Believing in yourself is always in your control. You can choose to believe or choose not to.

Loving yourself won't happen overnight. Especially if you've lived the opposite way your entire life. Start by creating the habit now. Science shows it takes 21 days to reprogram your brain to a new belief pattern. So, for the next three weeks try to love the cool things about yourself. For instance, try the mirror exercise for 21 days. Or try loving your personal sense of style, your laugh, or the distinct qualities of your face. Or try all of these for 21 days. Choose to be grateful for your personality because no one has the same personality as you do. We are all special in our own beautiful ways. You have your own unique essence. I have learned to love my own light- the way that I can be happy and full of joy like sunshine. Being grateful is a deep experience. Now if you are walking around only grateful for the external value of your T-shirt and not taking the time to appreciate where it came from, who made it, in what conditions, why you connect with it, what it represents for you internally, then your sense of gratitude will not be felt within. Try to feel gratitude, a deep feeling of appreciation within your soul. Gratitude can be subtle yet profound. Most of all, it is heartfelt.

I once saw a sign above a restaurant cash register that read "You can always find something to be grateful for."

*"Me coming into my mommy's life and passing on really changed*

*her. She truly desires to find meaningful things to be grateful for every day. After she witnessed my passing, she values how precious life is now and **real-eyes-es** how much value is found in life by being thankful and giving praises. She knows it's worth it now."*

Try it for three weeks. Every time you pick up your cell phone to text or check social media, remind yourself to find something to be thankful for. It can be something very small. Just look around you. There's always something around you in this abundant universe to be grateful for. Maybe it's the music playing in the background that's soothing your soul, the bright blue skies that you can see through the crack of the window giving you a sense of color and lightness in your day, maybe it's the joke you happened to overhear in the café. If you keep putting the thankful energy out there, you will start finding more things to be grateful for.

Your day will get only better and better. I remember walking home from a coffee shop one day and I made it a point to find things to be grateful for the entire walk. I kept feeling better and better, my vibes were so high. When I got to the block right before mine, I saw there was a group of people around. What I did not know was that they would offer me a whole plate of food. They said they were doing a cookout for the community. I had a great conversation with them and felt great for that sweet surprise. Sometimes in life, it's the little things. I could have taken any path to get home. But because my vibes were so high from giving thanks and praises, I attracted that good experience to me. At any given moment, challenge yourself to find reasons to be grateful. It can be a mother you saw playing with her little child. The joy they exude might make you smile. And boom, you found something to be grateful for.

I traveled to India with a wealthy girl who was a bit materialistic. She happened to be the one person whose luggage didn't arrive, and she boo-hoo cried for a few days. She was so sad because she wouldn't be able to wear any of her Lululemon outfits she bought for the trip. After her tantrum, she began a journey of her own, a deep, inner quest that was apparent to all and beautiful to witness. Not only did she have to swallow her pride and humble herself to borrow clothes, but she learned a valuable lesson: don't take anything for granted. She learned to value that there are more important things in life, like love. Moments that can't be bought... A month after the trip, I ran into her and asked her how she was doing. She told me that the trip to India had changed her life, that now she was grateful for everything. She said that even when she takes a shower, she is grateful for the clean, hot water.

Buddha said "When you realize how perfect everything is, you will tilt your head back and laugh at the sky." We're such drama queens sometimes, aren't we? I'm not suggesting that you dismiss your very dear feelings, no definitely have compassion for yourselves and feel what you need to feel. But sometimes, the way we overreact can be a bit comical. No matter how bad things may get, the sun will still come out to shine every single day. Even under the clouds, it's still there. If we have to wait extra-long in a line, if someone accidentally bumps into us, or if someone steals from us, we freak out and are ready to go to war. Why waste your energy on meaningless things? The next time something or someone stresses you out, ask yourself if it's really worth it. You were born to live your best possible life. You can choose to have an attitude of gratitude or a nasty attitude. Your pick. It's easy to get upset. It's easy to complain. Living a life of thankfulness, respect, love and peace can be challenging. Just because something can be challenging doesn't mean not to do it. You were born to conquer challenges. Don't sell yourself short. You're worth it.

At one point in my life, I truly believed it was me against the world. Not in a competitive sense. I don't believe we're here to compete against anyone. What I mean is that the cards life deals us can either break us or make us stronger. It has nothing to do with anyone else. It all depends on how you see yourself and play your hand. If something bad happens, it's up to you to overcome that challenge. As they say, everything that comes your way is either a blessing or a lesson.

Let's say you have an unexpected pregnancy. You can be grateful for that in the sense that you're going to bring a new life into the world. Many women never get that opportunity. Or let's say you want to be pregnant, and you keep trying without success. Maybe the Universe has something else in mind for you, such as getting your career grounded first. Or maybe you were unable to conceive at the moment because you needed to focus on other things in your life and that's okay. A lot of times it's important to be grateful for the timing of the Universe... especially through trust. Trusting the Universe is a great way to show It your appreciation. I have a few friends who were married for years, and they were trying extremely hard to have a baby, and they conceived when they gave up trying so hard, ten years later. So long as you are breathing, learning and building strength within, you always have a reason to be grateful. God forbid, your mom passes away tomorrow, you can be grateful that she wasn't taken away from you sooner, such as in your childhood which could have been worse. As bad as being stricken with grief may be, you can consciously choose to focus on the positives. Go through the motions and don't deny your sorrow but choose to find the good, the lesson... the silver lining.

The same goes for how you view yourself. You could sit here and complain about how much you dislike this or that about yourself. You can think you suck at a million things. You can think to yourself you'll never be great at anything, or you can give thanks for every single gift you do have. My grandmother always said, "everybody has something." You can be grateful for having a wonderful attitude towards life. You can be grateful for your sense of humor, even if it's quirky... I bet you've made people laugh before. You can be grateful for taking the time to go on a self-love journey- whatever that means for you. Cuz babe, no one will love you like you love you. This healthy attitude will lead you to even more gratitude. Better things will start to show up in your life. You'll find more and more things to be thankful for and you'll start to feel joy. And then more joy. You will begin to open up more to life because of such a thankful attitude.

I can list 25 things right now to be thankful for if I just take the time to think about it. I'm thankful for my passion. I'm thankful for my moments of peace, for hot soy chai tea latte, my favorite song, the beach, Mother Nature, water, food, transportation, friends, dancing, smiling, laughing, clothes, restrooms, perfume, yoga, the internet, cell phones, books, beds, compassion, love, flowers, memories. See how easy that was? When Bob Marley was asked if he was a rich man, he answered "When you say rich, what do you mean?" The man interviewing him asked "Do you have a lot of possessions?" Marley replied, "Do possessions make you rich? I don't have that type of richness. My richness is life. Forever." That was some real ass shit. You can have a million-dollar bank account and still feel so poor. You may be rich in ways you don't even **real-eyes**. You can breathe. Can you imagine not being able to take your next breath? God willing, you aren't suffering in pain right now. And if you are, trust- like everything else, this will pass. If you can put food in your mouth every day, you're not going hungry.

That is a blessing. Not everyone has the luxury of eating meals throughout the day. If you have a family you can depend on, you are far from poor.

I once met a guy on Skid Row named William. He went there every single Friday to serve free hot food to the homeless. "Skid Row serves the homeless food," he told me, "But they don't serve them good food. The food I'm giving them is good!" Every Christmas William works on a huge toy drive in the heart of South Central, California. When I asked him how he got into all of this, he said that he himself had been homeless. He'd told God, "If You ever deliver me from homelessness, I will give back." If only everyone had a heart like William's.

Buddha tells us to "give, even if you only have a little." There is so much profound beauty in giving. When you give, you feel rich. When you give, you are telling the Universe that you have enough. It is a way of showing that you trust in abundance- that you trust there is enough for all. William is far from rich. He's currently living with a friend in a pretty dangerous neighborhood. He could probably use some new clothes. But he believes he has enough to give back. To me, he is rich. His heart is gold. We are all rich in some shape or form. Whether it's the roof you have over your head, or your meaningful friendships, you have something others may not be fortunate enough to have. All you've got to do is just start to perceive your life as being fortunate, and you will **real-eyes** the fortune you do have. You will begin to feel happier and see that our world is actually abundant. It's about catching your mind up to the abundance that already exists within Mother Nature.

You can be grateful for anything that has ever happened, because it has made the world the world it is today. You can say the same thing about your life. You can be grateful for everything that has happened to you because it made you the person you are today. I look at my life and yes, there was a lot of trauma. There was a lot of low self-esteem and self-hatred because of it. *"My mommy was doing the best she could. She didn't have all the tools to help her believe in herself after all that she went through."* When I think about how far I have come and who I have become, I am blown away. Sure, I've still got more becoming to unfold but I wouldn't change who I am to be anyone else not in a million years. There are indescribable things that makes each of us unique cosmic entities full of the love we need right inside of us. Things about us that are so unique to our essence, we ought to give thanks and praise daily for our being alone. The truth is we don't need love from others to validate us and who we are. It's all within you and your soul. Keep believing in yourself and don't ever stop.

I believe in reincarnation. I don't want to keep learning the same lessons over and over in the next life or the one after that. To tell you the truth, I want to live my very best life in this one and evolve so I don't have to keep coming back. I want to move on to other levels and maybe come back as only a spirit guide to help guide others since we all have guides. I am beyond grateful for my spirit guides. They are the ones who point out the signs like crazy throughout our days. Sometimes you may read something or see something on the TV screen and then you hear that same exact word at the same exact time in a song. Those are confirmations that they are here with you, guiding you along. I am beyond grateful for them being in my life because they have helped me in so many situations. They have protected me and steered me in the right direction. Even when it didn't feel very good.

I'm thankful for the adversities, the trials, the struggles, the challenges. My life may not be perfect, but whose life is? That's not what it's about. I'm grateful for my immeasurable strength and the woman these experiences have shaped me into. If things had happened differently, I would not be the person I am today. You would not be the person you are today if it weren't for the things, you went through.

There have been times when finding the lesson was confusing. I fell head over heels for a boy and I couldn't get over him. He was the first guy to ever reject me, and I had no clue how to handle it. I lost my mind. I was heartbroken. I was sure this had happened to teach me a lesson, but I couldn't figure out what that lesson was. Recently, I **real-eyes-ed** that this rejection taught me to always love myself and never lose myself in someone else. It taught me what I truly wanted from a partner, and it taught me to never settle for less. I learned to love myself too much to care what anyone else thinks about me. If someone says I do this too much or that I'm not good enough or I don't have this quality or that quality, fuck 'em. Everyone has an opinion. But what does that matter when living my truth is the most important truth to me and my soul? As long as I love myself, you can suck balls and kick rocks.

Do I regret this love story from ever happening? No, because being rejected was a lesson I respect. I have to respect someone else's decision and I don't have to take it personally. It does not mean that I am bad or that something is wrong with me. Although it may have ended very painfully, for a time, I was madly in love and in total bliss. I can't find words to describe how beautiful this experience was before the pain came. I try to take the good with the bad and look at it all as another step on my journey.

I'm still learning to love myself more and more. The journey may be a little tough, it may seem never ending, but it is totally worth it. I deserve every bit of living the best and most fulfilled life possible, a life of self-love, respect and gratitude. Why in the world would I want to live any other way? Do your best each day to live a life of self-love and gratitude, and soon you'll look back on who you were before and compare that person to the person you are today, the person you've worked so hard to become. I think of life as climbing up a mountain. I had to start from the bottom, but I'm soaring up to the top. I believe that there is no end point when I'll say "That's it! I'm done!" No; I could be 98 years old on my death bed, learning more and growing more, finding more reasons to be thankful, and loving myself more deeply. As long as we're alive, there's more to learn. This life is truly ours to create, so why not choose to create one with meaning, depth and, most importantly, gratitude.

Start giving thanks and praises for your future self and your future life. Take the time to envision your new self and life. Feel it in your energy. Feel everything new. Literally draw up a new life for yourself. This is something we can all do at any moment. You are the creator of your life. Change your thoughts. Change your energy. Open up to the new life every new day.

# Practices/Affirmations
# for Giving Thanks and Praises

*Go a whole day truly, genuinely meaning "thank you," whenever you say it to someone.*

*Practice being thankful for even the simplest things. Even for a smile exchanged between you and a stranger.*

*Practice being grateful for all types of things for 30 days straight and see how you feel next month.*

*Give thanks to the Co-Creator/ Higher-Power/ The Universe, whatever faith you believe in.*

*If it does not bring a sense of sincere gratitude, I do not want to partake in it.*

*When things don't go your way (a special friend named Gerald Wilson taught me this,) pause and tell the Universe "Thank you," and switch your thoughts to something you do want instead. He calls this mind transmutations. Give yourself reasons to be thankful for who you were created to be. The person who resides inside of you, give reverence and gratitude for the unique essence that makes you you.*

*"I am grateful for everything." (And list things you are grateful for. Pause and connect with these things and why they're so meaningful to you).*

*Gratitude is a form of Abundance.*

*"I am so grateful for my incredible life." (Call it in. Claim it. Create it).*

## CHAPTER 3

# Is This Love

When I was eight months pregnant, I was sitting in Starbucks completing what I thought was the first draft of this book. At least that was my goal. My plan was to have my baby and then publish my book I had spent 3 years working on. As I sat there, there were customers stopping by to tell me I was about to pop. I was huge! One woman asked me if this was my first baby, and I said it was. She then yelled "You are going to die! You are going to die with love when you meet him! Just wait and see! You are going to DIE!"

Weeks later, on May 12, 2015, my spine was injected with morphine. At 5:30 pm as medication took effect, the doctors were ready to operate. Within 5 minutes I met the most beautiful person I have encountered in my life. The woman at Starbucks was right. I nearly died- with love. I saw my son Kamden Lee Efevberha for the first time. I screamed "Oh my God! He's so gorgeous! He's so Perfect! He has my lips!" The surgeon said, "I hope he has more of you than that." They took him off of me to be checked out and then the energy in the room shifted. Eight doctors hovered over him, and the tone went from chatty to silent. I was still pretty doped up; I was in and out. My mom was with me, and she is in the medical field. I heard her yell "what's wrong?" and they didn't respond. When I glanced over to see what was happening, I noticed that his body was blue from the neck down, and when the doctors lifted up his arms, they just flopped like spaghetti.

So many things were wrong when I thought about it. The whole operating room paused in silence as the pediatricians forcefully pressed their hands against his chest. *"My mommy deserved to have my life in her hands. I was not going to go out like that. Not with her as my mommy."* He let out his first cry ever. They shouted, "Ahhh! That's what we were waiting for!" I was barely coherent, but my motherly instincts kicked in. I felt something was wrong. The doctor who performed the Cesarean section went to go see what was going on.

The medical team resumed their chattering. They told me everything was fine and that they were going to clean him up. In the recovery room, my mind was filled with thoughts of my new little angel. I was still out of it, but excited at the same time. After a few hours, I was brought to my room, and they brought Kamden to me. *"I was so happy to be in my mommy's arms. I was happy about my grandma too."* He was sweet, chill, stunningly beautiful, had the best scent, and he was smart. He had the softest jet-black curly hair, golden skin, exquisite facial features, a high forehead, the most striking lips, and super long limbs. (His dad's profession was basketball.) Everyone commented on how stunningly beautiful he was. His energy instantly stole my heart. He was passionate and romantic. Pure love radiated through his being. If you met him, you'd see what I'm talking about.

After spending a few days of quality time with him, I had some concerns. My mom who worked in a hospital for over 30 years, was worried too. Something was wrong. After the first wail, Kamden never cried again. I asked the nurse "why are all the other new babies crying and mine isn't?" Let's say her name was Cindy... her response to all my questions was, "oh, that's nothing." Why isn't he opening his eyes? Why isn't he moving much? Why can't he eat anything?" I felt that the nurse was annoyed, that she thought I was just a new mom asking too many questions. Then the lactation nurses spent hours every day in my room, trying to get him to feed, but they couldn't figure out why he wasn't swallowing, even from the bottle. "*Nobody paid attention that something was wrong with me from the time I was born.*" Mind you, Kamden was a newborn, I had him in my care for 3 days straight with everyone insisting everything was fine, while at a star-studded Beverly Hills hospital for crying out loud! Kamden's eyes kept twitching, they never opened, and bubbly spit foamed from his mouth. Again, when I asked the nurse why, her response was the same, "oh, that's nothing."

The medical staff kept telling me that everything was fine, "he's just getting adjusted to the world," and like anyone, I believed them. The hospital had a stellar reputation, right? So, I kept dismissing my intuition that something was not right. On the second night of his life, he spent a few hours in the nursery. The next morning the nursery doctor came to my room to tell me that Kamden would have to be checked for neurological issues. She told me not to worry too much, because if it had been very serious, they would have rushed him to the E.R. a long time ago.

I went into panic mode. It was the most terrifying moment of my life. I felt like a truck had run over my soul. My mom and I had sensed that something was wrong. Especially my mom... Once she saw foam coming from his mouth, she kept asking the nurse as well because she works in the hospital and she knew that was not a good sign. But they kept dismissing her as well. Now he was being rushed to the Neonatal Intensive Care Unit. I overheard a doctor as another doctor "why is he being brought to us on his third day of life?" I was livid. Something had been wrong all along and nobody had paid attention! Talk about negligence. There had been plenty of red flags. Can you imagine if I took him home resting assured by their word that all was fine? His body flopping like loose spaghetti right after birth should have been enough. One of the doctors caring for Kamden in the NICU noticed his body jerking and moving strangely. She immediately knew he was having a seizure and they hooked him up to a monitor. Kamden was having 96 seizures per minute! The first protocol was to give him meds to try to slow the seizures down. Next was to find out what was causing the seizures.

They had to run so many tests on him. They pricked him in so many places because he was really in critical care. Waiting for results, not knowing what was wrong was horrible.

The instant Kamden was rushed to the NICU, I stepped into my role as a parent- immediately. I was facing every parent's worst nightmare. Every day he spent in the NICU was hell for me. In and out, day after day, hearing beep after beep from all the other little babies monitors. Seeing the pain on the parents' faces- I have never been in one room with so much intense pain. The agony on every parent's face was insane. I could feel the heavy energy. The angst, stress, worry, fear, hope, despair, denial, anger in the room was beyond measure. Parents would talk to me about their sleepless nights, wondering if they'd ever be able to take their baby home. I could relate.

I woke up every day, bright and early to spend time with my baby for as long as I could. I just sat watching him connected to all these wires, the head, the needles. I would hold his hand with my finger through the incubator. Kamden was a bad ass. Just a few days old and he showed me what a fighter looks like. For an entire month, I sat with him in the NICU, where I could (after his cast was removed from his head,) finally hold him for hours. I didn't even care that I had just had a C-section and I was not supposed to climb stairs... I went up and down my apartment's stairs every single day and night to spend all day with him. I only cared about being the best mommy I could be to my sweet baby. I spent most of my days pleading to God to just please let me take my baby home with me. I would hold him until they would tell me "You should go home and get some rest."

I dreaded going there every day, hated seeing his head wrapped in a cast attached to wires. It made me feel helpless. But at the same time, I felt powerful and full of strength, because I knew I could handle this. Considering all of my past trauma, they all had prepared me for this moment where I was facing the most difficult trauma of all. I also knew this was all beyond my control. I prayed a lot. I remember reading a bible verse asking Jesus to please heal him. I would randomly open up to bible pages and come across verses stating how the Father healed... I clearly remember envisioning Jesus laying hands over my baby to heal him; I was begging him. Yet in my clear vision, I saw Jesus surrounded in light, lay his hands full of bright white light over my baby's white casted head and body covered in white, but Kamden was not healed in my vision. I felt like I was under thousands of feet of dark water, and I couldn't breathe, like I was drowning. The pain ran so deep it's almost indescribable.

My mom stayed with me, and my family flew in to visit us. They all cried. My mother's crying shocked me the most. I'd never seen her cry in my entire life. If she cried, she hid it well. Even my grandma asked, "what's wrong with your mother? She doesn't cry." I knew I had to be strong for myself, my son and my mom. The doctors were very hopeful. Because it had taken him nine whole days to open his eyes. An ophthalmologist was called in to examine him. He told me Kamden's vision was good and that he looked healthy. Many doctors were hopeful, but boy were they wrong! The day he opened his eyes for the first time, he looked at me like no one had ever looked at me before, I felt like I knew those eyes from ages ago. I felt like his eyes knew me as well. His eyes were deep and beautiful and full of wisdom. I will never forget this moment.

On the 13th day of his life, he cried for the second time. At first, the nurses wouldn't let me hold him, this meant I could only stare at him in his incubator. Finally, I was able to hold him in the NICU for a few hours until the nurse had to put him back in his incubator to be changed. When she tried to take him from me, he held on with all of his might. When she pulled him away from my chest, his face turned bright red and he let out the biggest, cutest wail. I was in shock and so was the nurse. I started crying because he had finally cried and because he hadn't wanted to leave me. He knew me.

I tried to make the best of the situation. I sang to Kamden, so he'd know he knew his mommy was there with him. I sang my all-time favorite song, Bob Marley's "Is This Love?" When I was 15, I'd listened to that song over and over all day. Now, when I sang those sweet, sweet words in my baby's ears, I understood why that song had been my favorite. It fit the circumstances perfectly. I sang about how I wanted to love him and treat him right. How we'll be together every single day and night. I sang that I would take him home to my single bed that we would share and that Jah would provide the bread. "Is this love that I'm feeling? Cuz, I, I'm willing and able." At times, I felt like it was all a test of faith, preparing me to be the best mom I could be to him. I knew I was willing to do whatever I could to save Kamden's life. *"I loved hearing my mommy sing to me every day. It made me remember what it was like to hear her when I was in her belly. That's why I love music so much."* Whatever I could do to make my baby feel better. Anything to take him home from the hospital so we could finally start our lives. I wanted to give my little bubba all the love I could because I never felt a love so real; a love so pure.

For three weeks, the doctors could not discover what was wrong with Kamden. I held onto hope and faith. I learned what it meant to believe in the moment, and to have the utmost faith in God and what God wanted. HIS will for my baby. People told me to have faith, to believe that God would heal Kamden. But for me, faith meant accepting God's will, whatever it might be. I prayed constantly, I tried to envision Jesus Christ laying his healing hands on my son. While meditating on this vision, I saw Jesus sitting at a golden alter dressed in white with Kamden on his laps. My baby was dressed in white too, with a white cast covering his head. I tried with all my force to envision Jesus touching Kamden, laying a hand on him, lifting him up in the air- something! But I couldn't see it.

Every time I meditated on it; I saw only Jesus holding Kamden on his lap. The vision was very angelic, and Jesus was with my child... but it wasn't what I wanted to see. He still had his cast on. I wanted to see healing.

The library room at the NICU was equipped with amenities for the parents- cookies, coffee, magazines, computers, books. Books about babies with leukemia and brain malformations. Books you don't really hear too much about. Books about miscarriages and life after the loss of a baby. I saw those books and thought "Nah... that can't be me. Kamden's going to be okay, and I'll be able to take him home soon." The ceiling of the room was decorated with stars, each with the name of a child who had passed away in the NICU, donated by the grieving parents. "That won't be me," I thought. "Right? Right! No way! Of course, this isn't how my story goes."

A geneticist asked to meet with me, and as soon as he saw me, he started crying. He explained Kamden had been diagnosed with Zellweger's Syndrome. Zellweger's Syndrome is one of four in a group of a very terrible disorders called Peroxisome Biogenesis Disorder (PBD.) His was the most severe disorder of the four, and his life expectancy was the shortest. In milder cases of the disorder, children can live until their late teens, but in a vegetative state, suffering with uncontrollable seizures. There is usually no forewarning with this disorder, and it is extremely rare. It's so rare that there is no chance of survival, no cure, no option. I was like you've gotta be kidding me. I couldn't believe it.

I looked up Zellweger's Syndrome. Kamden had all the symptoms. One in 100,000 babies are born with a form of this syndrome, and the likelihood of me meeting someone else with this rare genetic trait was one out of 400,000. Kamden's life expectancy was less than one year as is most babies born with Zellweger's. The doctors gave him a prognosis to live for three months, max! They even gave me the option of "pulling the plug." They kept trying to explain to me that that would not be a death sentence, but I just couldn't do it. *"I'm so happy my mommy didn't do it. I was able to spend precious, unforgettable time with her."* I don't believe it's up to us to choose when someone dies.

A few days before I gave birth, I listened to a few chapters from Gary Zukav's "Seat of the Soul," in which he basically says that if a parent ends up losing a child, don't judge it because that was a contract both of their souls agreed upon before coming to Earth. I remember thinking, sure that makes sense but that would never happen to me. Of course, I'll have a healthy baby, I had been healthy my whole life and the baby's father was a professional athlete. When I got the news about my precious Kamden, I knew our souls must have signed a contract as Gary Zukav suggested. Interestingly enough, around this same time I had an aunt explain to me that "whenever you have a baby, it's not yours to keep. The baby is yours to borrow and it is a gift from God." I tried to accept the truth of what she was saying. Kamden may have come here for a quick entrance and exit, but the reality I was facing was grim. I would have to meet tragedy head-on.

I spent many days looking for inspiration, strength, and guidance from the Universe. How could I look on the brighter side of life at a time like this? When other parents in the NICU told me about their sleepless nights, I tried to cheer them up by comparing my story to theirs. I'd say "Yes, your child may have been premature but at least your baby has a chance at surviving. At least you get to take your baby home with you." Kamden's love got me through it all. "*I love my mommy so much. I knew every time she came in to see me. Every time she sang for me. Every time she held me. I love her so much. I wouldn't have had it any other way. This was the best way I could have spent my life. With her love and loving her.*" I knew my time with him was so short and that he could go at any given moment. I heard other parents complain about their babies. One woman told me she was going to give her baby up for adoption because the little girl had been born with a cleft lip. I could not believe what I was hearing. I was facing the fact that my baby was going to die in the near future, and you want to give yours away because of something as shallow as a cleft lip? Unbelievable!

Of all 25 babies in the NICU, mine was the only one who hadn't had a stroke or been born prematurely. He was the only baby in the room without a chance of making it out alive. That was my reality and I had to accept it. Every parent's worst fear is losing their child. That fear was my reality. I lived every single moment of every day in insane pain, and I had no choice but to hold on. Kamden had some serious fight in him. "*I have a lot of fight, but I got a lot of it from my mommy.*" He stuck through and I tried with all my might to fight with him, to make the best of this horrible tragedy.

The day I took him home, I was terrified. My mom and aunt had to both leave, so I knew I would be alone for the first time with him. I felt like I was walking on eggshells. He had so many seizures and I was all alone with him. I wanted a hug, something, someone to tell me that things were going to be okay. Watching him endure those seizures, I felt powerless. I learned what it meant not to be in control. But I couldn't freak out because I was all my precious baby had. "*I was happy she was all I had.*" All I could do was be there for him, breathe with him, tell him it's okay and hold him. Love on him.

We were blessed with the support of my loving family and friends. Family flew in and I usually was fortunate enough to have someone help with Kamden. We had several nurses who were all extremely loving towards him. In Kamden's third month of life, Nadia, my very best friend came to help me raise him. I was so grateful to have her with me and him. She cared for baby Kamden Lee like he was her own baby. Nadia is a transgendered woman who knows that, biologically, she can never bear her own children.

She laughed with him, fed him, blew his nose for him, and went to the ER with us when his biological dad declared he couldn't be there due to a "family emergency." If I ever needed to step out for my own sanity and as a healthy outlet, Nadia was there to watch Kamden for me. Nadia went on long walks with Kamden. She sang to him in the mornings. We were able to spend Thanksgiving and Christmas together with our Kam Bam. The mornings were filled with music, singing, dancing, prepping Kamden for his physical or speech therapy sessions, and the days continued with endless cuddles. *"The cuddles were my very favorite part."* Nadia and I nicknamed Kamden the "Cuddle King."

Eventually, his seizures became less frequent, and I was very grateful. In his first few days of life, he averaged 96 seizures a minute. By the time I brought him home, he was having 26 a day. Upwards three months of his life, he was having maybe four a day or none at all. At times, I didn't feel like I was even living. I was in a different dimension, but my times with Kamden were dope as fuck. Some of the most beautiful moments of my entire life were spent cuddling with my baby. We got so close just sitting with each other. He and I connected, we bonded. It was so intense because I held on to every moment as if it were his last. I never knew when the time would come, but I knew it was coming. So, my moments with him were blissful, and for that, I am blessed.

Our moments together were filled with the deepest love and the deepest pain I have ever known. Kamden was a cool dude, super chill, very aware of his surroundings. He was strong and confident. Even at his age, I knew his personality very well. He hated being very hot, but we had to keep him bundled up because had he caught a cold or pneumonia, he would have died. But, boy, he did not like covers on top of covers on top of pants and socks. He would always fight with his legs and somehow managed to get one leg out of the blanket to feel some cool air. He was very expressive with his lips. Both my mother and father made that comment about him when they saw his photos. His lips were stellar, and people always commented on them.

Whenever I would come home from running errands or taking a hike, he made really loud sounds, almost as though he were calling out to me. With as much pain and discomfort as Kamden went through, he seemed comfortable in his own skin. His demeanor seemed to say "Welp, this is me. I am me and I love me. I'm cool as shit! What?!" He seemed to have signed up for this life, and he handled it like a boss. I learned so much from that little fellow named Kamden Lee Efevberha.

He fought what he was facing with every ounce of his soul, with calm determination. He had a silent confidence, as though he effortlessly lived in trust. Although he was a newborn baby without the ability to know what was going on, he could feel things. He could endure intense pain, total discomfort and yet his attitude was very positive and chill. In the midst of it all, he was able to receive and give more love than I have ever known. I chose to engulf myself in every aspect of every moment with him.

I told him he was the cutest boy in the world, cradled him for hours (this is how we spent our days,) held on to every breath, every moment, every sound he made. I read to him, talked to him, hummed with him. I really, really enjoyed holding him and looking into his eyes, because that's when we felt the closest.

Kamden loved touch and music. He loved the water. When we poured water over his head to wash his hair, he looked like he was in heaven. He would reach out and rest his little head on my shoulder or my neck. Kamden's Zellweger's Syndrome made him very lethargic, so he would love his naps, and I just know he loved having them with his mommy. Kamden communicated with me in an extraordinary way. Although he didn't make sounds like a normal baby, he'd "Hmmh" and wait for me to make the same "Hmmh" sound back. We would go back and forth for about 30 minutes straight. Sometimes, in the middle of the night, he called for me by saying "Hmmh" and I'd say it back and forth with him until we fell asleep again. That was our thing. He may have been born with brain malformations, but he was very smart in his own way, very aware and alert. If someone.. to read: That was our thing. He may have been born with brain malformations, but he was very smart in his own way, very aware and alert. If someone came to visit, he would peek his eyes open and if he wasn't really into them, he went straight to sleep. The intensity of love for your first child is insane! Sometimes, the pain was just too much. Sometimes I hiked the steep canyons near my home, and I would fight suicidal thoughts. I looked over the edge of a cliff and **real-eyes-ed** I had the option of ending it all right then and there, and how simple all of that would be. The pain was that bad. I used to plead, "why not me? Why him?" I wanted so badly to be the one to die so my son could have a chance at living. As his mother, I just wanted to be with him. I thought, well if I jumped, we would at least be together. The thoughts were so real for me, I became afraid of heights. I wanted to end all the pain.

But I believe suicide is a cop out. I tried. I tried and tried and tried to be okay, to handle this situation the best way possible. I saw a therapist once a week and learned that my suicidal thoughts were normal given the circumstances. But I also knew that I had to try my very best to combat the depression. I had to face this like the biggest battle of my life. I had always been a fighter, and my ability to fight got stronger after Kamden was born. He had all the fight in the world within him, which inspired me. Every time suicidal thoughts came up, a higher voice within me would say "No." My inner self constantly told me I am strong enough to handle this. I told myself "I Can Do it." or, "I got this! I had conversations with myself about the fact that Kamden had not been born in vain. I would learn my lesson and find a way to live a happy life. Kamden would want that for his mommy. I knew that there was great reverence in his birth and death, and I focused on building my inner strength through meditation and positive affirmations. I looked in the mirror, into my own eyes and told myself to fight. Fight for Kamden, fight for myself, fight for my purpose. And I did. I kept on fighting with all my might and giving up was no longer an option for me. Kamden was the best example of what a fighter looked like.

My soul knew it had too much to live for. I didn't come here just to give up. There's too much love, too many lessons to be learned. I believe that if we miss life's lessons, they'll keep presenting themselves to us in different circumstances until we learn them. Love carried me through my experience with my son. I had loved ones who told me not to focus on Kamden's inevitable passing, but on the love, I could give him while he lived. I couldn't give him a long life full of promises. So, I overwhelmed him with all the love in my heart. I was able to make the best of a terrible situation, and although he is no longer with me, I know that he came here and received my love.

When Kamden was 9-months-old, I had to downsize to a studio apartment and could no longer live with Nadia. A close friend came to spend the night the same weekend I moved, so I put Kamden on a futon and shared the bed with my guest. I hadn't seen John in a few years, so I was more than happy about his visit, but at the same time, I missed sleeping in the same bed with my baby love. During the night Kamden's breathing became deeper than normal and he was coughing forcefully. I kept waking up to console him. His coughing would slow down and then come back. I told myself that if he was still coughing in the morning, I'd call the nurses to check on him. While I was switching his feeding tube, he placed his foot on the inside of my thigh. It felt like home, like one skin. He kept smiling at himself in the mirror near his bed. He smiled nonstop. Kamden had hardly ever smiled. With Zellweger's he physically couldn't smile all that much. Sometimes he'd crack a tiny smile after I gave him a big kiss on his cheek, or he'd smile in his sleep. But that night, he smiled continuously; blissfully. It made my heart so happy to see that.

The next morning, he seemed better because he wasn't coughing. But as I looked at him, I thought "wow, Vanessa, you're really taking care of a very sick baby." He looked and felt extra frail when I picked him up. Kamden made our "Hmmh" sound, and I kissed him and said "Hmmh" back. I drove my friend to the airport with Kamden in his car seat. John said goodbye to us both. He went in the back to say goodbye to Kamden. As soon as he got out of the car, I turned the music down and said "I love you, Bubba. I love you." Kamden went "Hmmh," and I went "Hmmh," and then he went "Hm-"it sounded abrupt. I said "Hmmh" again, but this time he was quiet. I figured he'd fallen asleep. When I got home, I took him out of the car and brought him inside. He'd looked extra sleepy in the car seat, but sometimes he got like that. Something was off. He was very light, very frail and he wasn't breathing loudly like he usually did. That's when I **real-eyes-ed** he wasn't breathing at all. "*I wanted to wait to say goodbye to mommy. So, I waited until she dropped her friend off so I could have that last moment with her.*" His lips were blue, his skin was very pale.

I freaked the fuck out. I was in disbelief saying "Oh no. Oh my God. Oh no." I knew this was going to happen, but I didn't know how it would feel at the moment. I tried to call my mom, but the calls kept dropping. When I finally reached her, she paused for a few moments, then calmly said "Ok. Call the ambulance." It was terrifying. I won't lie. I was alone and I wanted some comfort. It was all too much to take in. I called 911 countless times, but again, my calls kept dropping, and when I got through, they kept me on hold for way too long. Once I got on the line with a dispatcher, they directed me to give him CPR until the ambulance got there. I told him he had DNR in place and that he was in hospice, but they told me to try anyway.

So I tried. But I knew there was no hope. I knew it was over. But I was his mother. I tried everything I could. I followed the dispatcher's instructions, and I kept giving him CPR until I heard the sirens approach the complex. The police, ambulance, and fire department arrived. They checked Kamden out for a few minutes and then told me they had pronounced him as dead. "You don't believe it yet," the cop said. I didn't. I called my old roommates, and they arrived in just a few minutes by the grace of God. They were in shock, too. I ran to the bathroom and vomited. My body had gone into survival mode. My friend told me to give him a kiss as they laid him on the stretcher. I kissed my baby's blue lips for one final goodbye.

Looking at my dead son made me feel invincible. I was looking at the destiny everyone faces. His body may have decayed, and his physical life may have ended, but his soul lives on. Energy can't be created or destroyed. I believe souls go on after the body passes away. It gives me the confidence to know that my soul will go on. I didn't **real-eyes** it the day Kamden passed, but that day transformed me profoundly.

I have to take something good from this tragedy. We made a short film for Johnson & Johnson, to spread awareness of my son's rare fatal disorder and got 100,000's of thousands of views.

Kamden celebrated his birthday every month, and he was there for my 30. My friends flew out and talked to Kam, took photos with him. All this made my heart smile very much, and I'm sure he smiled, as well. Kamden was loved immensely. My family pitched in and made sure we were financially stable since the dad was not in the picture and I couldn't work, knowing my baby could go at any moment. His dad met him only a handful of times, but many people loved on Kam Kam, and he loved on them. His heart was humongous- maybe it was too good for this world.

Kamden's funeral was beautiful. I left early as that is the custom in our family heritage. I had family members fly internationally and help console me. I felt blessed and comforted. But it was hard. I remember driving to the cemetery one night and I just yelled uncontrollably. Until the security told me I had to leave. I wanted my baby, here with me.

Nadia moved back to Florida, and I moved to Colorado for grad school which I will speak about later, but three ½ years after Kamden passed away, Nadia passed away right before her 34th birthday. I miss her dearly and she is still a guiding force in my life and will forever be my best friend, but I am grateful they are together with each other right now. I wouldn't want anyone else taking care of him. Since I saw how she loved on him like he was hers, I am grateful they both have each other on the other side and they are cheering me on together on this side. I have two beautiful angels guiding and guarding me. They are my baby-loves and I cannot wait to see them again.

*"We are always with you and inside of you. Whenever you think of us, we are there- we are here."*

I gave myself permission to grieve, but still, I chose to focus on the good. We were built to live here in this world, and with life comes painful experiences. As I fought my pain, I felt very alive. It made me face life and ask myself if it was worth fighting for. I decided to fight for my happiness. Fight to feel alive. We are here to win in life. Whatever winning means to your soul is the reason you are here now.

# Practices /Affirmations
# to Choose Love After Adversity

*Whatever happens in your life- trust. Trust that this is happening for reasons only your soul and Source may be aware of.*

*Know that there is always worse out there. No matter how bad things may get.*

*Cherish every precious, present moment you are gifted with. You never know when life will end.*

*Honor your unique journey, even the painful moments. They make you see yourself for who you really are.*

*Live in love. Choose not to live in any other way. Always choose love.*

*When life gets tough, know it's a signal to be gentle with yourself.*

*Live each day with passion and purpose.*

*"I am a survivor, I thrive."*

*"I live a resilient life.*

*"I am powerful, no matter what happens."*

CHAPTER 4

# Love the Life You Live, Live the Life You Love

So, you live your life, and everything is fine. Then all of a sudden it rains. It doesn't just rain, it- storms. We all know what happens after it rains right? The sun comes out, and sometimes there's even a beautiful rainbow in the sky. But what happens when you don't know how to live happily anymore? You got so used to the rain that you think it's still raining, even in the midst of sunshine. We can get addicted to sadness or negative circumstances, forgetting that life can brighten up. After my hellish experience was over, when I finally faced my childhood trauma, I kept thinking that life was still bad, that things would still go wrong. "*It took her a while to move forward. But we try to help her. All of us guardians help our loved ones from the other side.*" I had gotten used to focusing on what would go wrong instead of simply letting life happen. I believed that only bad things would come my way, but life takes its own course. I had a friend recently tell me that things usually don't turn out the way we ever expect it to. Sometimes it's good, sometimes it's bad. But most of the time it is never as bad as we think it will be and it is the complete opposite of what we do think it will be. In all reality, it's all about how we look at it. Anything that we experience can seem to be bad if we choose to look at it that way.

You always have the option of believing that a bad experience came along to make you stronger on your path, to help your soul evolve.

I used to think that good things wouldn't happen to me. I had become so accustomed to the bad moments in my life- that doubt underlined most of what I did. I lived in the belief that everyone was out to get me, and I was trapped in a negative thinking. In order to think positively, I had to build a muscle, exercise my ability to view a situation as good, no matter how bad it might seem. *"When you know it's painful and you feel it hurt, that's how you know it's time to try your hardest to focus on the good."* To think positively is to look forward with optimism, no matter what the past has shown you. Limiting yourself to what you have experienced in the past, without allowing the possibility for change; you have no room for growth, for truth. Change takes place constantly, but we leave ourselves no room to recognize it. Isn't it crazy to live as though the past is still happening? If you keep doing the same things you have always done, you'll get the same results. If we were meant to live in the past, we would still be there and there would be no such thing as the present moment.

Some of us are stuck in the past. A guy once told me that his sedated grandmother yelled in agony about four different occurrences in her past. She could never let go of the past pain. She screamed as though she were a four- year- old arguing with her mom. I don't want to be like that when I am in my seventies. I see "mentally ill," people yelling in the streets all the time. The reality is that the past is gone and if you don't let it go, it will follow you to the present, preventing you from living fully in the moment. I'm so guilty of this. It takes constant practice to make living fully in the present moment a habit. I find that the more I attempt to live in the moment, the easier it becomes.

# WHY WORRY?

Worrying takes time away from your life. In moments of worry there is only fear. The opposite of worry is trust. Which do you choose? It's so easy to worry about what could go wrong. We tend to forget about how often things do work out in our favor. Patience plays a big part. For example, it would not be wise for me to worry about how I'm going to pay the bills when I haven't received a phone call about the jobs I recently applied for. I have to wait a few days before I can call them back to check on the status of my applications. I can choose to freak out or to trust that things will work out in due time. While I'm waiting, I'll apply for more jobs, and if none of that works, I'll call the bill collector to ask for an extension. I always have the choice of living in fear or living in trust and love.

If I choose to worry, my problems will remain the same and my life will be miserable. It's about learning the art of control to the extent that you can be able to allow life to take its course. What sense does it make to choose the option of worry? Everything changes, so whatever is bothering you will not go on forever. Now never goes on forever. Who knows, if you put enough good energy out there, you just might find what you were missing. That car accident might bring you a check for a new car. Dude, just go with the flow, and see what happens next, because the next "next," is coming. For you

108

never, ever know. As the saying by Greek philosopher Heraclitus goes, "change is the only constant in life." At 25 when I suffered from severe- anxiety attacks, I knew it wouldn't be like that for the rest of my life, and that perspective helped me cope with it.

# FEEL THE HURT

Life will move on with or without you, whether you want it to or not. Do you think that when you pass away the whole world will just stop? It's beautiful that people have loved you and will continue loving you and will truly miss you. But life goes on. Life is alive and infinite. The question is, how are you going to choose to live? How are you going to deal with your stress? Are you going to let it kill you, or are you going to kill it? The battle is real. What matters is how you face stress and deal with it. Remember, this is your life, and you can always choose how to live it.

Too often we deal with something that feels unbearable as though it will last forever, and we push the feelings away. (I will speak about this later in chapter 10.) We may think we're escaping the pain, but it's inside us. We think we're living a happy-go-lucky life, but the sadness still lives there. The best gift you can give yourself is the gift of feeling. Feel the rage, the anger, the sadness, the hurt. Only once you've felt it, can you overcome it. Feelings are not facts, and they are definitely not permanent. Thank God, right? Feel the jealousy, feel the passion, and feel the fear. But feel all of these feelings with awareness. Become so present that you fully feel. Get curious about your feelings and ask yourself where they are coming from. "*When you feel your feelings, you can feel so much more of yourself and what YOU feel like.*" When you do this, you allow yourself to fully feel the next fleeting feeling. And then the next. If you are aware of your feelings, they can't get the best of you. You are allowing life to take its course. Let's say you hear a nostalgic song that brings you back to a painful breakup with the love of your life. The first thing you might do is change the song to get rid of that painful feeling. But if you simply let the feeling come and pass through you, it will heal. You will accept it for what it is.

I'm not suggesting it will not hurt. Sometimes your feelings will hurt like hell. But you are strong enough to handle them. You are stronger than you think you are. Everyone is. Don't let sorrow and pain get the best of you. Even in your own anguish, you can remember what good feels like. Don't fall into the trap of sulking in your sorrow. You can kiss your internal wounds and put bandages on them in the same way you would a flesh wound.

*"I love when my mommy takes the time to heal by looking through her feelings and accepting everything as it was, because then she can let things go and transcend."*

Truly experiencing your feelings will allow you to become aware of yourself and who you are. You will see how strong you actually are when you stop running away. And the best part is you will become emotionally mature- emotionally intelligent. Emotionally intelligent people face their feelings and choose to take care of themselves appropriately.

You cannot control how you feel. Your feelings are a very real part of who you are, so why not honor them? Stand up for how you feel. I never knew how to accept my feelings, especially the dark ones. But a therapist taught me to acknowledge them and to speak to myself about them, to tell myself "I understand how you feel right now, but I will take care of you." During my time in India, whenever I meditated, I felt an excruciating pain in my heart, and I couldn't understand why. I decided not to run away from stabbing pain. I said to myself "you know what? I'm going to look at you. Instead of being confused about what you are, I'm going to go deeper." I decided to feel the pain even more. What I found when I looked really deep within, was that I was harboring the pain of a past betrayal. I looked at that incident from the depths of my heart and admitted to myself that it hurt like hell. In that moment, I decided to feel the pain. It wasn't pretty. It was scary as fuck. Who wants to really feel pain? Especially intense emotional pain. But I attained liberation that night in India. I was no longer a slave of the pain that someone had caused me. I accepted the hurt for what it was, and I **real-eyes-ed** there was a gift for me in it.. The gift of forgiveness. The more you forgive, the more of yourself you attain. Can you imagine spending your life looking for revenge? Some people do. But it is never about the other person or the incident. It's always about you and your journey. It's about how you learn to live from that moment on. It's about growth.

I'm learning that allowing life to go on and being able to move forward from an intense experience is a challenging process, something that requires fortitude. You have to consciously choose to let go of all that has happened. And that may take a multitude of attempts. It may take a multitude of events of mind fucking yourself into understanding and believing that you have a brand-new future ahead of you. It's about acknowledging what has happened and being able to tell yourself you are going to just let it go.

When you choose acceptance and forgiveness, you give yourself the gifts of freedom and self-love. Hanging on to resentment is a form of self-violence. It imprisons you. Forgiveness is something you do for yourself. It can involve coming to terms with truth. What is the point of living angrily about something that already happened? Why hold on to those terrible feelings? Forgiveness is a gift of healing your precious heart, so that it may become whole again one day. It's not one of those things you say once, and it's done. Resentment may come up again and again and every time it does, you have to forgive again. But in the process, you recover part of yourself, and you grow. You not only get stronger, but you become lighter and more open to all that life has in store for you. Forgiveness means loving yourself and valuing what's important in your life. I don't believe you can forgive without finding compassion for those who have wronged you- not by pitying them, but by placing yourself in their shoes and trying to understand that they may be hurting deep down and don't know any other way to exist. Hurt people hurt people. What someone does to you is never personal. If someone harms you, they are going through a serious battle within themselves. What they truly need is love.

Some say before we were born, we signed a contract (as I mentioned earlier), agreeing that we are here to play a role so that we may grow and learn. If you believe that everything that happens in life is a lesson, going through a few painful bumps won't matter much and you can enjoy the show from a higher mental standpoint. When you understand that whatever happens contributes to the evolution of your soul, you'll stop fighting the lemons life may throw at you. If God is love and love is the Creator, then why wouldn't we be the creations of love? It's easier to grasp life's lessons when you're not busy complaining about how terrible it is. Once you take everything that happens as a blessing, you can begin to appreciate your unique journey and life becomes sweeter.

# STOP STRUGGLING AND START DANCING

Learn to look at the colors around you. Look at the different shades the light makes. *"Look for the signs, we send our loved one's signs all the time if they are paying attention to the simple things."* Notice the feathers you may come across or the person's name who was just mentioned in the song as you were thinking of them. Notice how time is passing. Listen to all the sounds. Notice everything that moves and everything that is still. Watch the sky change as the day goes by. Smell the air and notice the different aromas and how they change. Feel the weight of the air when you walk into a room. Watch the looks in people's eyes as they pass you by or while in conversation. Smile for crying out loud! Pay attention to your breath. Take the time to eat slowly, to really enjoy the taste of your food and drink. Listen extra carefully when people speak. Learn to ask them questions about what they've said so you can practice being alert and interested. Stop getting lost in the noise inside your head. Everything happening in your head is not all in the present moment. Just what is present is present. Activate your senses and choose to live every moment to its fullest.

Try this practice randomly throughout the day: imagine what your soul looks like, what it's doing. You may witness your soul in a dance position, in a slay warrior position, in a seated meditation pose, in a jumping jack, in a fetal curl. All of these images reflect what's going on within your soul at the moment. I invite you to bring this into your life on a regular basis and connect to what your soul is expressing- as your soul is tied to your truth.

Albert Einstein said, "true religion is real living; living with all one's soul, with all one's goodness and righteousness." Notice how you feel when you allow yourself to slow down and really be in that moment. See what happens when you allow yourself to be totally present. Your spirit becomes alive! When you fully allow a feeling to come and then go, life opens up a little bit more, even in your darkest hour. Life is a dance. The more you can align yourself with the beauty all around you, the more you melt into the flow of life. The Japanese might say life has a "yugen," meaning the emotions we can't quite grasp that relate to the mystery and beauty of the universe. When you are present in the here and now, an ever-changing molecular phenomenon occurs. This is life's flow; the ever-present calm on a river.

Hey, hey, hey, don't sweat that incident. It's only in your mind. A new moment is coming, and after that, another one will come. What just happened may have been a hidden blessing in ways that you cannot see just yet. And there's hope for what may come later in the day. When you allow yourself to melt into the present and flow, you truly feel alive.

# Practices/ Affirmations to Move on with Life

*Embrace and accept the fact that nothing lasts forever.*

*"I welcome with open arms all that life has in store for me."*

*"Life is always on my side."*

*Move with every new moment as it comes along.*

*Practice being present every chance you get.*

*Consciously choose to let go of the past- often. Almost use it as a self-cleansing process. This works very well during lying- down meditation.*

*Try new things so you can embrace the ever- present newness of life.*

*Inhale the "new," exhale the "bull shit."*

**Real-eyes** *that every moment is new.*

CHAPTER 5

# Could You Be Loved

You're given a body, a family of some sort, air to breathe and a world to live in. But do you ever really know who you are? Do you know who truly lies at the core of your being? Have you ever asked yourself, "Who am I?" and then pondered what the answer is or could be? You might think, "I'm Jim. I'm five feet ten inches tall. I'm a singer in the making, and I'm from Ohio. I like to eat Korean food, grill steaks, and drink beers with my boys while we watch football." You may describe yourself like that and think that's who you are. If you're an actor, a doctor, a customer service rep, you may identify much of who you are according to what you do. I used to think I was a college graduate with a degree in Public Relations who didn't know what path to take to match the desires of her heart. I used to think it did not matter much that people thought I was attractive. I identified as a light-skinned Haitian girl from North Miami who grew up without a dad and didn't know how to show her feelings. I thought people would be annoyed if I displayed self-confidence, that they might hurt me or make fun of me. I was sure that others wouldn't be supportive if I was just myself.

Do you really know who you are? Not the person you want others to think you are, or even the person *you* think you think you are. Who are you, really?

Maybe you think you're the stories you've been telling people about yourself. But that's not the answer. You're not the transgender person you have chosen as your identity. You're so much more than that. You can't come close to describing all you truly are.

I think the best word we can use to identify ourselves is "soul." We are each a soul, and a soul is infinite. A soul simply is. And it's grand beyond human understanding. If we are infinite beings, how can we wrap our minds around all that we are? Try to identify yourself with your soul rather than with the identity you've given yourself, or the identity you think society has given you. The closer you get to your soul, the closer you will be to your identity, your true essence. And your true essence is AMAZING!  You are a magnificent, magnanimous being. When you do things from your soul, other people really dig that shit. Try it. Learn to listen to your soul. It will lead you to your true self.

By getting close to my own soul and really getting to know it, I've discovered who I truly am. I've shaved my head, let my hair grow into dreadlocks, not because something consciously told me to do so, but because my soul made that decision. It led and I followed. Shaving my head was an expression of my soul in that time and space. If you listen, your soul will lead you to make the right career choice, make friends, express who you are by how you dress — anything, everything. Even if it takes years to finally hear what your soul is saying, if you keep listening and following, you're sure to find it.

The old adage "Just follow your heart" is wise. Love is the key to hearing what your soul is telling you, because your soul resides there. Listen to your soul, and you'll lose the need to live up to society's expectations and imposed definitions of success and failure. Stay tuned-in to your soul and you'll operate from a place of love.

Is it scary to live this way? Yes, it's terrifying to go up against society's norms. But listen to your soul, anyway. If you're feeling a bit lost, trying to find yourself, listen to what your soul has to say to you moment to moment. Then set your soul free.

# CHOOSE TO LIVE FREELY

By choosing to live freely, you can become more closely aligned with your path. Each of us has a specific path, although we can take different routes to get there. Following your soul's calling is the way to find out who you are at your core.

Self-realization or **real-eyes-ing** who you truly are, is a matter of allowing yourself to unfold naturally. I've spent years trying to figure this one out, and to be honest, I'm still on the path of discovering who I am. I say "discovering" because it's a continuous process, a constant exploration, an endless adventure. So far, I've been successful in this quest of **real-eyes-ing** my true self, not because I'm a genius or special, but because I never gave up searching within. Quite frankly, I don't have it all figured out, and I don't think anyone on Earth does. I don't care who you are. I'm only here to share what I've learned so I can help others believe in themselves and who they uniquely are.

I'm a lot closer to knowing who I am now than I was before for one reason: I never gave up searching. I know it takes work, an internal digging to understand who you are. This journey is ongoing. Life, in itself, is a journey, a very specific journey of constantly allowing yourself to be who you authentically are.

# SOME PEOPLE BRING OUT THE BEST IN YOU

I have no clue who I am and yet deep within me, I know exactly who I am. Do you ever feel like that? Have you ever met someone who brought out all your soul? The crazy in you? The good, the bad, the intellectual, the beautiful, the bizarre, the talkative, the funny, the unpredictable you? The fully expressed version of you? Those are my favorite people. In their company, I find that most of myself is revealed to me. I feel free, expansive, like the rawest version of myself and I get a glimpse of whoever this "me" is. Choose to hang around people who bring out the best in you.

I once met a guy who drove me crazy. I yelled. I did dumb things on purpose. I talked his head off. I was comfortable around him, one hundred percent authentically me. How many people get close enough to see you for who you truly are? The real you? How often are you authentic and vulnerable, sharing your real identity with others? Most people only see what you want them to see, because most of us are wearing masks. I didn't last very long with that guy, but in those few moments I was with him, I was astonished to meet the person he brought out of me.

I love that we are here on the Earth to play specific roles, especially to play the role of revealing our true selves. Others can be our mirrors, revealing who we are. Can you imagine what it would be like trying to discover yourself in a world with only you? With no one to share yourself? Others help us by reflecting our souls.

Think about the times you've fallen in love. You weren't necessarily in love with the person in front of you, but you absolutely loved who you were when you were with them. I was probably the most in love with my ex, not because he was a legendary musician, but because he understood me. He accepted me for me and allowed me to simply, freely be myself. He embraced me wholeheartedly and gave me a safe space to express myself. He hardly spoke. I did most of the talking. But he listened, totally alert, aware, and accepting of me. He was right there with me, never judging me.

They say that the most healing gift you can give anyone is to be present when you are with them. To meet them with total awareness. They say you don't have to talk to heal someone. You can heal by just being there, fully, wholly and acceptingly.

I love all my cousins very much, but one of them brings out my truest self the most often. We're like soul sisters. Anyone who can open you up and make you feel like a blooming flower is an amazingly beautiful human being. I love our experiences and conversations together. She is very opinionated, and I respect that. She doesn't ever start a debate for competitive purposes, but she leaves room for open conversation, personal exploration if you will

— so I can think and be curious. She leaves room for me to search deep within my being, to explore what my deepest truths are and to freely express them without fear of being judged.

When you lose the fear of being judged, you become your truest version of yourself. You're no longer wearing a mask or putting up barriers to block your identity. Ask yourself, "Who have I felt the most comfortable with?" Then think about how you were with that person. Not necessarily how you treated them or vice versa, but who you were when you were around them: totally comfortable, totally free, totally you! Ask yourself if you can be that way with everyone you encounter. I challenge you to open your heart to those you meet, and shine, baby, shine! No matter what.

I understand the fear of being rejected, the fear of getting hurt for revealing too much of yourself. I understand judging yourself, being overly critical of yourself. And I'm not suggesting that you reveal all of yourself to everyone. I believe in boundaries and keeping certain parts of yourself for yourself. It depends on how much your Higher-Self suggests you reveal to others. But if you're not being yourself, who are you posing as? And for whom? I still struggle with that. I had a huge fear of being rejected for my light, until I **real-eyes-ed** that the very thing I was afraid to share is what makes me unique.

I choose not to live in fear of rejection. When you trust your soul, your gut, you know how to gage how much of yourself to reveal. When you let your soul run the show, it will not steer you in the wrong direction. You will get guidance from your soul about whom to trust and whom to be comfortable with. A lot of the work is learning to trust your soul, to trust that it knows. It will guide you to understand which people are good for you and which are not.

Yes, I'm suggesting that you allow yourself to be vulnerable. You have nothing to lose, and you will gain a part of yourself not easily accessed: your soul. I don't believe we were born to hide ourselves or to give bits and pieces of ourselves to others. I believe we were born to embrace who we are. If you choose to live without resisting who you truly are, you can set your soul free. You'll discover a flow, an ease, and a way of being. You'll engage in a dialogue with your soul, and with the universe.

# Simply Be Who You Are

The journey toward finding yourself has a lot to do with simply being who you really are, not the person who does things to impress others, or buys all the latest designer clothing in order to feel better about themselves. This type of person masks their insecurity with material things in an attempt to compensate for what they feel they lack. Your true self is not a person who hides who they truly are because they feel they aren't good enough. Or an arrogant person who hides their insecurity by boasting about how great they are and explaining why others should love them.

In today's society, we are taught to be a certain way in order to be accepted or deemed successful. I kept people in my life who I knew weren't good for me in order to feel liked and accepted. If we can let that need go, we could take on forms that go against this. The true individual can express who they are without apologizing for it or trying to prove a point. The true expression of the soul is much grander than the personifications we choose.

People tried to make me feel bad because I wore sexy clothes, although I lived in tropical Miami. I didn't post photos on social media in order to gain acceptance. I might be fully clothed in one photo and half naked in the next. Now I go with my own flow and march to the beat of my own drum. I have found self-confidence, a love of my soul and inner being, which needs to express itself in its own ways. Maybe a year from now, I'll get tired of wearing sexy clothes and want to dress more conservatively. But I am not willing to change how I present myself based on what someone else thinks of me. I have my own journey to walk.

People will often judge you for what they cannot understand, what they cannot label easily, or put into a box, and this may come off as extremely demeaning. For example, my very close transgender friend Nadia is regularly ostracized, mocked and ridiculed. Others find it difficult to understand that a person can be born in the body of one gender, while having the soul of another. When I am with her, I hear dirty remarks being thrown at her. Yet clearly, she is just living her life as the person she is.

Sometimes people close to you try to control you. Why? You don't fit into any of the boxes they consider "normal." Recently, a childhood friend told me that she thinks I've changed, which I don't think is bad at all. She said that she doesn't want me out here looking like a girl who doesn't come from a good family, since I do. I was confused because she was shaming me for the way I chose to dress. She didn't like seeing the half-naked Vanessa. But it's my body, isn't it? I believe that as long as you're not hurting anyone, you should be true to yourself.

Until you can love yourself for who you truly are, you will

constantly seek approval and acceptance from others. Finding yourself is a process of stripping away everything you use to identify yourself with that isn't who you truly are. This process of stripping away all that's not you may be hard, because it forces you to face your inner depths in a brutally honest way. But there is beauty in that. Why come to Earth to live a lie? Why not get to know yourself and be true to the inner voice that lies within you?

To know yourself is a privilege and a blessing. You are magic! It's a huge reason why you're here. Being who you truly are is a beautiful artistic expression of your true essence.

# Perfection Doesn't Exist

Why do we assume that we have to be perfect? Think of the talks you've had over dinner with people you thought you had to impress. Everyone has had these experiences, whether it's a gathering, a business meeting, a classroom, or an event. If you've ever felt the need to "do things right" to avoid being rejected or ridiculed, know that fear exists because you have rejected yourself. If you totally accepted yourself, would it matter if someone else didn't accept you? No! You'd still have yourself, the one thing you can never lose. Sure, we all like applause at times. Appreciation affirms our existence and reminds us that we are loveable. But we don't need to be validated by others, liked by all, and hold the attention of most. Fuck all that shit!

We try to live up to our false ideas of ourselves when we're not completely honest about who we are. It becomes an unconscious habit. You get used to putting on the mask, the clothes that cover our true selves and we play pretend. We become imposters. I was a pro at this. But when I began asking myself to be honest, I came undone. I'd become fed up with striving for perfection and decided to find out who I truly was. I **real-eyes-ed** it was perfectly fine to be imperfect and began to accept who I truly was. I stopped trying so hard and started to feel more comfortable in my own skin, more comfortable with my true self. I began to let my shoulders relax, to walk to my very own beat, to think for myself and value the things I truly value. I began to find my voice. My life and my focus became more about pleasing myself and less about pleasing other people. I put myself first. Not in a selfish way but in a self-respectful way.

# LISTEN TO YOUR SOUL

You lose yourself when your focus is all about pleasing others. We see people pleasers all the time, and we find it hard to respect them because they don't respect themselves. I met a girl who could see that I was very self–conscious and masking it like crazy. She repeated over and over, "Fuck people!" Do what's best for you. As comedian Kevin Hart says "Do you, boo boo! Do you." I'm going to do me. I'm going to listen to my own soul because my soul signed up to come here! I'll allow myself to be inspired by others but that's about it! I'm doing me, listening to *me*!

I've found that when you put pleasing yourself first, you care for others more. The way you treat yourself mirrors the way you treat others. And it teaches others how to treat you. If you respect yourself a lot, you will respect others, and vice versa. If you listen to yourself, you will become a better listener. When you love yourself, you love others. If you take great care of yourself, you will want to care more for others. Take the time to put yourself first. Give yourself the self-love, self-respect, and self-care you deserve, the self-love you may have needed when you were a kid. Then focus on respecting, loving, and caring for others. Your cup has got to be full first before you can focus on giving to others. So go on the journey of learning how to put yourself first and love yourself first. Learn about yourself, your inner self. Your soul. You're you for infinity.

Maybe it's weird that I like bright flowers and sunsets, meditation, reggae, yoga and chai tea. That's my thing. *My* thing. Sure, I'm obsessed with reggae music. I can listen to it all day long. I love burning incense and dancing to rap music. That's my thing. I love quirky things, like watching kids play and people smile. That positive energy makes me happy. I love having random conversations with random people because I learn so much. I love helping people look at the bright side of things because it could always be worse. I love digging within myself for past patterns that may be the cause of my current neurosis. I enjoy digging into the root of the issue, pulling it out and victoriously moving on with my life. I love learning lessons and evolving. These are the beauties of being alive.

# Just Let Life Happen

This journey won't be completed overnight. Our souls are here for eternity. I once spent an entire summer trying different things so I could find what I truly loved. I was like the Jim Carrey movie "Yes Man." I said yes to every chance to try something new. I went roller blading to see if I liked that. I went to the zoo. Once I stopped searching so hard, the answers came. When I just let life happen, sat back, and allowed things to be; life was sweeter. I began to learn more about myself. I'm still learning. It's a beautiful unfolding. When you focus on the present moment, there will always be more, more unfolding, more of you to discover. Your soul is ever expansive and eternal. But your life is not eternal. You only have one chance to live this gift.

Before I could get comfortable with myself, I had to get comfortable with life, with everything happening around me, the things I cannot control. And I had to get comfortable with the critics, with their opinions of me, their misconceptions. I had to learn not to let their conceptions of me get to me — ever. There will always be critics, and they will not always know what they're talking about. One of the most liberating truths that came to me during a spiritual experience is that I felt, while taking a sensational shower, that no one in the world has the answer to anything. This means that there is no limit to what you can create or perceive. It was liberating to **real-eyes** that no one else's thoughts are necessarily better than my own. It's entirely up to me to decide if someone's perception of me is accurate or not.

# TEACH OTHERS HOW TO TREAT YOU

I had to accept that criticism will always exist, but how I choose to deal with it is completely up to me. Growing up in a Haitian household, I let those things get to me. Everyone was concerned about what the other family members would think. I'm human, it still happens sometimes, but people's negative opinions often have nothing to do with you at all. My suggestion is to first ask yourself "Where is this coming from? Is this coming from a place of love?" A lot of times people say things to you to hurt you or bring you down because they're so hurt themselves. Most of the time this is unintentional, and they're unaware of it. It's up to you to ask them what they mean, teach them how to treat you. It's a way of standing up for yourself by using your voice, or silently with your body language. Silence sometimes speaks much louder than words.

I was treated by a therapist who specialized in childhood sexual abuse. He told me that if someone said something I found offensive, I should repeat what they said and then ask them what they meant. For example, if someone says "Vanessa, you seem so slow." I would say "I seem slow to you? What do you mean?" Nine times out of ten they won't able to give you a valid explanation, and they'll become aware that their comment was out of line. Ultimately, it's what you do with the information that matters. People will push your buttons. It's up to you to decide what's true for you, whether you let someone's words knock you down, stand up for yourself, or dismiss it because it doesn't ring true.

# A Blessing or a Lesson

I believe that life offers us certain truths about ourselves, and I think of those moments as growing pains. Let's say someone tells you something that really bothers you because you know it's true. But what do you do with this truthful information? Beat yourself up? Feel sorry for yourself? Defend yourself with denial? Maybe you're mortified that someone has seen that side of you, so you lie about it. You convince yourself and them that it's not true, which doesn't serve you at all. I believe that when these negative pointers come your way, they offer a chance to see a reflection of yourself. They mirror what's really going on and allow you to only take a deeper look within. If you can avoid beating yourself up, you'll have an opportunity to evolve and become a better person. Yes, it may hurt, that's why I call these moments growing pains. The journey may feel very uncomfortable at times but consider it a gift, an opportunity to get intimate with yourself, to discover how you really feel about things.

What do you do when someone tells you that you don't know how to be a friend and that you will end up alone if you don't learn how to show respect to those who love you? This happened to me once. Boy, that was a tough pill to swallow! I allowed myself to feel the pain. It hurt badly, but I had a choice. I could have chosen either to sulk and hate myself or get to work and become a better person.

There's a saying that "Everything in your life comes to you as either a blessing or a lesson." I received those hurtful words as both. I think everything can be both a blessing and a lesson. But I also believe that if we fail to learn the lesson, the lesson will be presented to us again and again. Notice how the same lesson presents itself to you until you learn what the lesson is. I understand how discouraging it may be. You may feel you're not good enough and your inner critic may beat you up.

# YOU ARE LIMITLESS

Deep down in the depths of your soul there is limitless potential. That's where the truth that "nothing is impossible" resides. When you think, "I just can't do it," you can choose to find the deeper truth, which is yes, yes you can do it! You can do whatever it is you put your mind to, even when every cell of your body, mind and spirit feels like you cannot. There are no limits to the truth of who you are and who you can become, which is why it's so important to keep your inner critic in check and slay all the shit it's talking about when it gets out of line. When you see that your inner voice has nothing constructive to tell you, it's time to redirect and start praising yourself. Seriously, this inner battle and dialogue is very real. It's your responsibility to keep it positive and stay full of love for yourself and others.

Some truths come to us, when we least expect them. They can be positive, like "Sandy, your character is so impressive. You always seem to go above and beyond for your loved ones." This can be a positive reminder to keep doing what you're doing because it's blessing others. These beautiful reminders should never be forgotten or taken for granted. These are the things that will matter to us on our death beds when we ask ourselves how well we lived our lives. Was I a beautiful person? Did I give my life meaning?

Did I help others find meaning in their lives? Did I appreciate the experience of living?

Both negative and positive comments that hit your soul can be considered useful truths. Your soul knows the truth when it hears it. What you do with the information is up to you. And this includes the bull people give you, which has no value because you know it's not true. In those moments, you acknowledge that this person's opinion doesn't matter because it doesn't relate to you and doesn't affect you in any way. Why would someone else know more about you than you know yourself? If people speak badly about you, don't take it personally, because you and only you, truly know your truth.

Each of us is dynamic, unique, mysterious. What a beautiful reality. I believe it's up to us to stand up for ourselves. Self-empowerment is learning to own your power and not give it to others. A classic example is when you react to something someone says about you. Or you react to someone's behavior. Not knowing how to respond in certain situations can be a form of not standing in your power. You are in control of your response to everything that happens. If you don't like what someone tells you, don't tolerate it and don't believe it. It's your life and your choice.

# STAND IN YOUR POWER

Who are you to tell me about me? Especially if you don't know me. Especially if it's not coming from a loving place at an appropriate time that will be useful to me? You've gotta learn how to tune into your intuition to understand what people's motives are and whether they're coming from a good place or not. The harsh reality is that we live in a world full of people who have ill will and cruel intentions. Most of the time, they aren't even aware of it.

People who are afraid of you will try to tell you about yourself. People who want a false sense of power and control will attempt to take your power away, especially if they feel you threaten them. They use everything they've got to make themselves feel more powerful than you are! And you have only yourself to blame if you allow this to happen. It's up to you to live your life to the fullest regardless of other people's opinions. You weren't born to compete with the person next to you. The minute you start focusing on what someone else is doing, you put yourself beneath them. The real competition is with yourself. Focus on yourself. Stand in your power. Stand your ground. I'm still learning how to do this. It takes time, but it's worth the fight. It comes down to knowing exactly who you are and standing in that truth in that moment. But to do this, you need to be truthful with yourself on a constant basis.

Two acquaintances once decided to tell me that I didn't know how to use my power when it came to men. They suggested that some women are smart with their power with men, implying that I am not. Who are they to tell me about what I know how to do with my power? And what do they know about what I am doing in privately with men?

I choose not to use my power to manipulate men. I could do that, but that's not who I am. I'm not competing to be the "most beautiful girl in the world." I may be attractive, but I don't strut my stuff. No one is entitled to tell you how to do what you do. We live in a world with many opinionated people, but it gets on my nerves when someone tries to bring me down. I could have beaten myself up and agreed, told myself "Vanessa, you don't know how to use your power with men." But because I know myself, I chose not to let it get to me. It's up to me to choose how to react.

I took their remarks as an opportunity to reflect on what I do with my beauty, and to ask myself what beauty really means to me. I asked myself and continue to ask myself to define my truth. I looked within myself and **real-eyes-ed** that I've chosen not to let what others think about me affect me.

Sometimes, people want you to change; sometimes they want to control you; and a lot of times, they consciously or unconsciously want to hurt you. They want you to live according to their terms.

# THE LESSON IN A CURSE

I was once extremely close with a girl I'll call Shelly who told me she was going to show me the world. And she did. We went to yacht parties in South Beach, woke up in penthouses, jet-setted a few times. I was twenty-two years old, and as happy as can be, wild and free. What I didn't **real-eyes** is that you can't always tell others when great things happen to you. The infamous green-eyed monster comes out, and we live in a world full of psychopaths and sociopaths. I was naïve. I thought others had my best interests at heart, and since I wished nothing but good for others, I assumed everyone else did, too. But I was wrong. I had to learn that lesson the hard way.

Shelly was a beautiful girl on the outside, and smart. So smart, she was cunning. She knew how to make people like her. She knew when to laugh to make people feel accepted and admired. What I didn't know about her is that she had to feel she was the best one in the room. She couldn't stand it if someone got more attention than she did. Later, I discovered that she'd grown up a middle child, always craving the attention her family didn't give her. They focused on the eldest child and the youngest, because she was so smart and always got good grades, whereas her siblings did not. I had no idea that I was dining with the enemy — a snake.

I began dating a very well-known guy. He had everything she would have ever wanted in a man. Little did I know that she hated me for dating him. So much so that she wanted me dead and in the grave. When I started noticing her envy, I distanced myself from her, completely stopped talking to her. I **real-eyes-ed** she had an evil dark side. What really surprised me though, was that several psychics told me she had paid a Bruja one hundred thousand dollars to put a curse on me so I would not be able to have children. She'd been selling drugs, paying cash for cars. She'd become used to getting what she wanted. It was probably nothing for her to give a black magic witch lady my photo. She might have thought no one would find out; but think again.

The first person who told me about the curse was an Indian man gifted with psychic ability. He told me to stay close to God and to my family. The next day, I was in the shower listening to a great reggae/Rastafarian song: "If Jah is standing by my side, then why should I be afraid?" when my brother called to tell me that our mom had been rushed to the ICU. She'd been involved in a freak accident. Four other people had been involved, but no one else had a scratch on them. My mom was severely injured, and although she recovered within three months, she'd fractured six ribs, and was bleeding in her brain. My soul was ripped open. To see my mother like that killed me. I listened over and over to Kanye's song "What doesn't kill you only makes you stronger." If the Indian psychic hadn't told me to stay close to my family, I don't know that I would have been as supportive as I was. Because he told me that, I chose to be at my mother's bedside every single day. This taught me what family is about.

Another of the psychics who told me about Shelly's curse told me she'd tried to poison me so I wouldn't be able to get pregnant. I guess the thought of me getting pregnant by that famous guy killed her, so she took extreme measures. When I became pregnant with Kamden, I was shocked. I may not believe in the practice of black magic, but know it exists. The day before my scheduled C-section to deliver Kamden, a very weird thing happened. I'd been in the living room with my mother and as soon as I went to my room to rest, we heard a loud noise. I went back to the living room to be sure my mom was okay. I asked, "What was that?" She said she didn't know, but it had come from outside and something hit the window. When I looked at the living room window, right smack in the center was a wet stain left by something that had hit the glass. When we took a careful look at the ground, we saw a dead, bleeding pigeon. My Haitian mom is superstitious. She called her sister to ask what this could mean. Then she cleaned the window, and I went back to my room. For the rest of the day, I didn't feel my baby moving, although he'd previously been moving a lot.

Later, I discovered through YouTube videos that some African cultures who practice black magic send a possessed pigeon anywhere in the world to deliver a death sentence. The cursed person may randomly get into a fatal accident or develop stage-four cancer. Whether you believe in these things or not doesn't matter, they go on.

After my baby Kamden passed away from his fatal disease, a third psychic told me that this Shelly had also put a curse on me around the loss of a baby. I was speechless. For my own sanity, and since I still consider myself a mother, I decided not to associate her with my son's death. It would have been too much to bear. Deep down, I knew it was true, but I also knew that some things are part of God's higher purpose. We may go through something utterly devastating so that God can propel us to where He wants us to go. You never know whose life you will touch with your story or why the Creator allows things to happen the way they do.

Three months after my mom's car accident another psychic confirmed all this by explaining that Shelly was psychotic and had spent twenty-seven thousand dollars to put yet another curse on me. I was devastated. I had nightmares about her shooting me in the face. I began to pray a lot more. I was already close to God, the Universe, whatever you want to call that ultimate consciousness, but now I was determined to get closer to the Higher-Power. I knew that human power could never compete with the power of God the Creator. I looked at the Earth around me and told myself that if the Creator had the capacity to create mountains, human beings, love within us, then surely, no human spell could match that.

When I felt low, I'd repeat a bible verse that helped me feel I could overcome anything, Romans 8:31 "If God is for us, then who can be against us? Who will bring any charge against those whom God has chosen? It is God who justifies. Who then condemns? No one. Who shall separate us from the love of Christ? Shall trouble or hardship or persecution or famine or nakedness or anger or sword? No, in all these things we are more than conquerors through Him who loved us. For I am convinced that neither death nor life, neither angels nor demons, neither the present nor the future, nor any powers, neither height nor depth, nor anything else in all creation, will be able to separate us from the love of God that is in Christ Jesus our Lord."

I used to add "nor any powers man does with his own two hands." This verse saved me so much heartache. It gave me power and faith in myself and in my relationship with the Higher-power.

Surprisingly, it brought me closer to myself. Over the years, I **real-eyes-ed** how weak Shelly must have been to go to those lengths. How insecure she truly was and how evil her heart was. I grew to have compassion for her. And I grew to have more respect for myself, so I wouldn't attract someone like her again. It also taught me that not everyone is for you, even if they act like they are.

# TRUST YOUR INSTINCTS

Living in California, it's not that hard to meet someone who grew up gang banging. A guy who used to gang bang told me, "People say actions speak louder than words, but really actions don't matter. Because you could just be acting. What really matters is the intention behind the action. How the person is really feeling." I was like, damn! That is so real! Being betrayed to that extent allowed me to **real-eyes** that people you are close to may not always have the best intentions toward you. You may have the best intentions, so you think their intentions are equally pure, but people can betray you when you least expect it.

A lot of us are too wounded and afraid to take a hard look at ourselves, which is why it's so important to have your radar on, to read the energy around you. Being betrayed taught me to learn to trust my instincts more and look into people's hearts. It taught me to look beyond the friendship, and to instead examine the person, to observe their headspace, spiritual space, and reactions.

What gets me about people betraying each other is that we all know wrong from right. Perhaps someone is so consumed by selfishness, they don't understand that their actions will affect someone else. They may believe they will gain something by their behavior, but by injuring a loved one, they lose much more. People who go around betraying others for their selfish gains are not well. They need prayers, love, and compassion. They are hurting so badly that they cannot see how they are hurting others. Or they see and they don't care.

Karma is a real bitch, and she will pay you back hard. She will teach you a lesson to keep you from acting foolishly and recklessly. Little does the betrayer know that they are prolonging their own journey. They take steps backwards. Whatever you put out, the Universe receives and will reflect that energy back to you in some form. Sometimes we know not what we do. We're unaware of the way our behaviors may affect someone. But let's be real. Why go down that dark route?

# FORGIVENESS IS A RELEASE

My experience helped me to stand within my own power. It forced me to search within myself, to know and understand that I won't give my power away. In order to stand within your own power, you must know what it means to be who you are and what you believe in, to live your truth regardless of what others do, say, think, or feel about you. You can stand firmly in your power by practicing forgiveness, practicing compassion for those who have hurt or betrayed you because you see that they are lost.

Hurting others is a form of hatred, the opposite of love. Tell yourself, "Tomorrow is a new day. Tomorrow I'll be the bigger person, do what's best for me and walk away, because I can no longer trust this person whose toxic presence is in my life. I'll choose to forgive, because by forgiving I am loving myself and not harboring any of their negativity. My forgiveness is a release for me. By doing so, I'll step into my power." The more you practice it, the better you'll become at standing firm, but this may require you to step out of your comfort zone.

# BE PRESENT WITHIN YOURSELF

Sometimes all it takes is being present. As Eckhart Tolle writes, "The past has no power over the present moment." When we don't focus on our past hurts, they have little power over us. Let it go and be done with it. You give your power to whatever you focus on. It isn't happening now, is it? Being present is the only way you can stand firm in your power, but a lot of people are not comfortable with it.

By being present within yourself, you avoid getting caught in the monkey mind of yours, jumping from thought to thought. That part of your mind can control you. And it's crazy! It wonders what the others are thinking about you, what they've done to you. The monkey mind can take you away from who you really are. Only negative emotions come from this mindless way of thinking. You may start to feel low in energy, angry, worried, anxious, afraid. Pay attention to the worries your mind creates moment to moment. How much anxiety and fear may be underlying your everyday activities. None of this is rational. Right now, you are a perfectly fine human being.

The first week after moving to California, I met a guy who told me he was a Grammy award- winning song writer for Katy Perry. I looked him up later that day and it was true. He told me that even huge celebrities like Katy Perry get caught up in the circle of fear. He'd have to go to the back of the studio to help relieve her fears. Everyone struggles with this, because when you're not fully present you cannot stand in your true power.

You cannot be centered within yourself and trust that you are okay just the way you are. Most worries make no sense at all. When I lost my sweet, precious Kamden, and held the dead body of my first-born son, I learned something very profound: What people think about you doesn't matter at all. Your soul leaves this Earth all alone. So, please, give me one reason why you should be consumed with what others think of you.

If loved ones have critical advice for you, consider it. But don't sit there and worry about what others think of you.

# GET REAL WITH YOURSELF

This morning, I spoke to one of the most amazing human beings I've met. I've known Adrian Christopher McClean for ten years now. He's an amazing fitness trainer— positive, loving, pure and such a vital life force. I could go on. What made our conversation so amazing is that he was giving me precious jewels about being who you are and believing in yourself. He told me that he'd started from zero. He began with a clean slate and learned to love himself deeply. People always compliment him on his positive, motivating, infectious energy. He **real-eyes-ed** that that was his difference. He told me how he got real with himself about it and used it as a starting point for learning to love himself. He told me how he approached others and the world around him. It was eye-opening. I immediately thought about how people constantly compliment me on the thing that makes me different. For me, it's my pure and genuine heart, an excellent starting point for learning to love myself more and **real-eyes-ing** that what makes me different can be a beautiful weapon.

Society doesn't teach us to give ourselves credit. It's almost as if we live in a world where we're shunned for believing in ourselves. Let's say someone walks into a coffee shop believing they're the shit. Let's say they're attractive, well-spoken and supremely confident. People may start acting funny, talking shit to each other about the person who just walked in. They might give that person dirty looks. The whole vibe changes. I don't understand why we don't support an attitude of self-love. No, damnit, it should be praised. Reciprocate that same loving energy. Love on them some, and love on you, too. Why not? There's enough love to go around!

I'm not talking about arrogance. I'm talking about truly loving ourselves and our lives. Learn to dig deep and get in tune with the uncomfortable aspects of yourself. Learn to fully embrace your totality. And choose to feel good about it all. I lived most of my life not giving myself the credit I deserved, and no one can give that back to me. If you like to be chill, learn to love that about yourself. Love what's different about you. Love those traits that make you unique. In this way, you'll learn to be happy within your life. **Real-eyes** that no one else can ever be you and you can never be anyone else. Would you really rather be someone else? All that glitters is not gold. And everyone who looks happy on the outside is not necessarily happy on the inside.

Understand that the Universe created a divine essence and unique energy that is you. Breathe into this deep knowing with reverence and honor yourself and your soul. The things that make you tick, the things that give you burning fire. Let your life be a free expression of who you are.

If you feel like posting something on your social media, post it. If you feel like being a singer, be one. If you feel like dressing in a certain way, do so. You get my drift? Stop giving a fuck and do you. At the end of the day, what others think about you will not matter. We're all going to exit this place called Earth. Let go of all the labels we place on ourselves, all the worries, the self-conscious thoughts. Don't worry if others think you're not pretty enough, strong enough, smart enough. Your life is not about living for other people. It's about being true to yourself and living your journey the way you choose.

# Choose Your Own Path

Recently, I was at a park with a girlfriend. We were going for a spiritual quest and exploration within ourselves. On the way to the trail, we got a bit lost and asked a guy we came across if he knew which way we should go. His response was so trippy! He was like, "I don't know. There are many paths you can take." And then he winked at us. It was one of those subliminal messages. You know, you can take tons of paths. It's up to you, which way you go. It's not about choosing the path others want for you, or changing who you are so that others will accept you and like you. Your life is 100% yours to live. If you're not being true to yourself, who are you being true to?

Society doesn't make this process easy. It constantly throws things in our faces, billboards displaying super-thin, Photoshopped models. The people we see on television have been glammed up and the message is that you should be perfect. In the Black community, there's a huge stigma among women. Not many Black celebrities have natural hair. The message is that we need to wear long hair extensions. Same thing goes for Caucasian women and dyed hair. The images on magazine covers, on the internet... my list could go on and on. What ever happened to looking natural? Choose the way you choose to be, whether it's "natural" or not. By all means, dye your hair, get extensions, and have fun with what you like. But do it because your soul is calling you to do so, not because you're mindlessly copying something you saw on TV or in a magazine.

Same goes for men watching music videos or commercials and feeling they have to be "flashy" in order to get the "hot babe." Whatever happened to men and women getting with each other because they genuinely like each other for who they are? There's a saying that "Whoever controls the television, controls you." Pay attention to how society expects you to be, versus the true calling in your soul that tells you how you want to be. I can't even imagine how colorful our lives would be if we each vibed to our own thing.

I can't stand that we all strive to be perfect. We try to live up to false ideas of ourselves, instead of being totally honest about who we are. It's exhausting and can lead to feelings of unworthiness. We're all equal. We bleed, breathe, have feelings, shit, sleep, work, die just like everyone else. So, how in the world does it make sense to live for other people? If you make it a habit to be dishonest with others in your everyday life, you're lying to yourself.

Babies seem to know this truth. Kids are not self-conscious about silly things like their appearance, language or behavior. They aren't afraid to speak. They scream when they wanna scream and say what they feel when they feel it. They speak their truths, always. Babies are probably the most confident beings on Earth. They're simply happy to be alive. They just live as if they are perfectly fine just the way they are. But we grow up in the school called life. Society teaches us how we should or should not behave, how to dress, how to speak, which neighborhood is nicer, which car is better... You get the point.

# FEAR RULES US OR WE RULE FEAR

You want to come off a certain way. First you convince yourself, then you begin to build a false sense of confidence around that idea of yourself. But this is not true self-confidence, because this vision of yourself didn't come from connecting with who you really are. You created it because you were afraid that you weren't good enough to be loved for exactly who you are. You created a role to play. Let's say you're an attractive woman who gets her hair done, wears Prada shoes, and carries an expensive handbag. She feels great because she looks a certain way and gets compliments. She may have made herself look appealing, but this is not where true confidence comes from. Anything you use to feel better about yourself that is outside of yourself is not true confidence. It's a mask hiding a deep insecurity worn by someone starving for validation, attention and, ultimately, love.

The approval and attention she may get from these external things won't make her truly happy. They won't fill the void within and make her feel fulfilled. The only thing that will ever fulfill us is self-love. The confidence you learn to find within will make you feel whole, truly loved, and at one with yourself. We were born without the absurd desire to gain other people's approval. We were born free to be ourselves, comfortable with who we are. Are you free now? Or are you tied up, just pretending to be free? True freedom lies within. What are you afraid of?

The fear of being hurt or rejected overcomes you when you reject yourself. If you totally accepted yourself, what would it matter if someone didn't like you?

I was a pro at this. It wasn't until I began asking myself to be honest that I began to come undone. Come to yourself. Come undone. Even if it feels impossible. Come to **real-eyes** that no one said you have to be perfect. You convinced yourself based on how you think others see you. Stop trying to be what you are not, and you might find out that you're perfect just the way you are. Once you become solid, content and self-validating, you'll exude confidence. You won't need superficial things to make you an acceptable human being.

Your inner essence is worthy! Your soul is valuable! You are an infinite being of Divine light! Always question where your confidence is coming from? If it's coming from a place of feeling good about who you are, or from the superficial things that society taught you to need.

Go to the place within you that doesn't need other people's approval, the place that unconditionally approves of you for who you are, where your Higher-Self resides. This is the way to self-love. Deep down you know this. It seems scary because most people don't take this route, and you have not been taught to go there. But this is the route to fulfillment, to living your life fully according to your own rules, because you are no longer living to please others. Rather, you begin to honor your truth. Learn to get comfortable with yourself, your surroundings, your decisions, your beliefs, your feelings and your thoughts.

You are the most important being in the world because at the end of the day, you have to die with the person you were born to be, the person you sleep with every night of your life, the person who never leaves your side, even if you try to run away. So, fight to be who you are, whatever you are, proudly.

It took me forever to get where I am now. I had to move some serious mountains and fight like hell. But I wasn't ready or willing to lose myself. You never know when you're fully there. I always feel like I have so much more to learn. But I know that I'm with myself, living according to my own rules, not living out of fear.

I'm not saying there are never moments when I feel fear. I constantly battle it, but I make sure I win, and I always win through love, through coming to my heart. Let's say I'm afraid of intimidating people with my beauty. I've been living with that fear for years because I was sexually abused as a child. But I consciously choose to come from a loving place. I decided not to hide myself, to come from a place of choice and healing. I choose to live boldly by embracing my beauty. I constantly enter untraveled territories and I don't let fear of the unknown rule my life. I go where I'm uncomfortable. Because in life, either fear rules us or we rule fear.

Someone once said something very wise to me: "Vanessa, if you don't have a gun in your face, why are you afraid?" He explained that fear can actually serve us in moments of danger, but unless we might be physically hurt, we shouldn't be afraid. When I thought about it, I was like OMG! He is so right! One of the most frightening moments in my life was when I was robbed at gunpoint. So, whenever I catch myself becoming afraid out of nowhere, I am like, "Wait a minute, Vanessa. Do you have a gun pointing at you right now? Is this something that's going to hurt you?" If my answer is "no," I stop being afraid. Like dude, why am I afraid to be myself? Knowing I came into the world alone and will leave it alone, why would I be afraid? Is appearing a certain way to a certain person something scary? Get the fuck out of here! That does not make any sense, does it?

I believe we were born to conquer ourselves and to conquer the fear that tries to stop us from being who we really are, the fear that tries to stop us from dreaming and pursuing our goals. To **real-eyes** that fear isn't real, each of us needs to regard our lives as sacred.

When I was in India, my guru told us to ask ourselves regularly, "Am I reverent with life?" Are you? How often do we just live our lives without noticing the beauty within our grasp at every moment? It's so easy to get caught up in our heads and block out all that's around us. The narratives consume us, the irrational thought patterns, when life is simply taking its natural course.

Why let fear consume you when love is present? The more I conquer fear in my life, the more I'm capable of living my life in accordance with love. Life is love. God is love. Love is all around us. We are love. Why would I want to live in its opposite form?

# Practices/ Affirmations to Embrace the Unique Art that is You

*"Don't judge, just love."*

*Discover what makes you unique and wear that swag with confidence. Honor those qualities within yourself.*

*Practice being self-confident. It is a muscle you build.*

*Find different ways to express yourself. Explore them and stick to the ones that make you feel best, such as painting, dancing, knitting, singing — anything that allows your inner voice to come out in a positive light.*

*Go with the flow of your soul.*

CHAPTER 6

# Be True to You

We all want things like success, nice cars, new clothes. We want to look "good." And success can look different to each of us. Most people define success based on external measures. But we also want certain things within ourselves. Maybe we want them even more than material things. The material things are fleeting. We use them to get attention and be liked. Dressing up in new clothes feels good. I'd be lying if I said otherwise. We desire these external things because we think they will make us feel good inside. But true happiness is a different form of success. What matters is not how we look on the outside. The internal things are much more valuable because most of our lives take place within. We experience life internally.

# LIFE TAKES PLACE ON THE INSIDE

The great speaker and author Ora Nadrich once said that "all of our lives take place on the inside. We see things and interact with things on the outside because we are physical beings living in a physical plane, but everything we experience, we experience within ourselves."

Your soul lives on for eternity. Everything on the outside will eventually fade. External things cannot fulfill you. They may make you feel happy, but only for a little while, and they can be taken away at any moment. But what lies within will only leave you if you choose to turn away from it. The external is always fleeting, always changing, while the internal is who we are. It is where love resides.

The desire for external things comes from a deeper place, for a deeper reason than you suspect. The deeper yearnings of your soul are the lessons you came to Earth to learn. Your soul wants to express itself in its full language and potential. It's not by chance that you want to live a happier life, that you want self-confidence, self- love, self- respect, patience. Maybe you want to be a more giving person, a humbler person, a nicer person. Whatever moves you is your calling. By wanting these things, your soul is communicating with you. Listen. Something deep within you wants you to evolve. 1 think we are all here to grow. If you learn to listen and follow your soul, it will lead you in the direction of your growth. Everything in nature is constantly evolving. It's in our nature to want to evolve and develop ourselves into high-performing human beings. The potential is limitless.

You can do something no one else can. You are a specifically designed human being with a unique soul and unique energy. So why in hell wouldn't you use every ounce of your soul to let this version of yourself shine? Why wouldn't you give your all to be the person you came here to become? You were born for a reason. Only you know that reason deep down within you. You were born with people around you not only so that you could experience love, but also so that you could discover qualities within others that you may want within yourself.

# JEALOUSY ONLY HURTS THE JEALOUS.

You may see something you'd like to have in a person, such as confidence. Maybe you'd like to have more of that trait, but that's no reason to hate the person who has it. It's the universe showing you what your soul truly desires and telling you that you can have it. If someone else can be confident, you can, too! Jealousy is a sign that you need to look within, that you need to discover what your heart truly desires. Use jealousy as inspiration to look within.

Remember to stay in your lane. Listen to the callings within you and follow them. Your desires are unique and should be honored. No two people experience exactly the same callings in exactly the same exact way. Nothing is more beautiful than authenticity, which is love in its rawest form, a reflection of your soul. It is deep self-acceptance. Sure, you could try to copy others, but would that be true to you? Most people live lies. They don't know how to be their authentic selves. But we are all born being ourselves. Every child is authentic until they forget how to be themselves. Most people don't know how to live the lives they truly desire. But when we listen to the inner callings of our desires, we find true fulfilment and peace.

# Living a Lie

Let's say you want to be bold and outspoken, but you're shy and live quietly, hiding who you really are. When you ask yourself why, you **real-eyes** that you are afraid of what others may think of you.

For the longest time, I was quiet. I didn't think I was living a lie because I wasn't pretending to be like someone else. But I was hiding who I was. I didn't want to come off as a nice, sweet girl who likes to smile. I thought I'd get too many envious stares or be judged and rejected.  I didn't want to stand up in my beauty, because I was afraid people would hate me for believing I was "gorgeous." It shocks me that our culture teaches us it's a crime to feel good about yourself.

By hiding these qualities, I was hiding myself, denying who I was. I didn't speak up when I wanted to say something or get up when I wanted to leave a room. I was hiding my authentic identity, trying to please people who could care less about who I was.,

Only when you live from the seat of your soul are you fully alive and liberated. Ralph Waldo Emerson said, "To be yourself in a world that is constantly trying to make you something else is the greatest accomplishment." I'll be damned if on my deathbed I regret something as stupid as not living my truth, not showing my light and living for myself because I feared what others would think of me. On my death bed, I want to be proud and happy about the life I chose to live. I want to go out knowing that I did everything I wanted to do, and I didn't give three fucks about what others thought.

Dude, if you want to feel like you are the shit, but you're afraid, you're only fooling yourself. You have no clue what they will think. More than likely they are so self-absorbed, they aren't thinking about you at all. You owe your life to yourself, regardless of what other people think about you. Focus on a Higher-Power instead. At the very least, you deserve to believe you are worthy of attaining what your heart truly desires. Napoleon Hill wrote, "The starting point of all achievement is desire. Whatever the mind can conceive and believe, it can achieve."

Your desires are unique to you for a reason... and you need to make those desires a reality. If you don't go hard to attain what your heart truly desires, then I'm sorry my friend, but you are living a lie.

I've always admired an assertive voice. I never liked hearing my voice crack or sound too emotional. The opposite of this is a strong, assertive voice that demands respect. It's natural to desire admirable qualities you see in others. Possessing a quality like assertiveness is much more fulfilling than wanting to possess something material like a Mercedes Benz. Once you get the Benz, what happens? It gets old and you're no longer as happy as you were when you first got it. The satisfaction you get from material things is fleeting. Whereas real magic happens when you work at improving yourself.

Because I wanted to sound assertive, I began adding more bass to the tone of my voice. I became more aware of times when I didn't sound assertive, and I'd consciously try to add assertiveness to my tone, whether it was with the cashier at the supermarket, at work, or on the phone with a friend. I slowly but surely became more assertive. I attained something I'd desired!

# ACCOMPLISH THE DIFFICULT

Look at what humans have attained over the course of history. There's no limit to what you can accomplish. It takes time, determination and faith. You may think attaining something you desire is hard, but you can just as easily decide it's easy If you choose to think it's going to be difficult, use that thought to your advantage. Get a thrill out of accomplishing the difficult.

Just do it. Put in the work. Challenge yourself, then choose to feel good about your accomplishment. Celebrate your win. We are such powerful beings, why not use our power?

Be free, independent, and true to yourself. Don't let the fear of being judged rule your life. My mom often said, "No way would I waste my time on social media looking at other people's lives. I have my own life to live." Break down the boundaries in your life. Do everything you can do. Experiment and take risks.

A wise artist named Jonathan Bickart said, "Five hundred years ago, people were doing things we would think were absolutely bizarre. I'm sure five hundred years from now, the things we're thinking and doing will seem absolutely ridiculous!" So. if you randomly want to go to the zoo, go. If you want to learn to crochet, take a class. If you are inspired to paint something, try it! Ask yourself what it is you truly want. Then go out and get it. Dude! If you want to drink, go for it. If you want to approach that hot babe, do it! And whatever happens, don't take the outcome personally. This is life, not a trial.

I'm all for envisioning beforehand, seeing the picture clearly in your mind. But if you spend a lot of time daydreaming that you can be the next Mr. Don Dadda and take no steps to actually be "that Dude," you're living a lie. If you create an image on social media in order to give a certain impression of your life and who you are, that, too, is living a lie. Does what people think about you hold that much weight? Are you living an illusion to convince yourself that you're something you're not? You owe it to yourself to be all you can be. And for no one but yourself. Only then can you begin truly serving others.

A friend of mine recently posted a photo on social media with this caption: "You don't have to like me. That's my job."

You've got to go hard, man! Go hard for yourself. Think about all the "greats" who ever lived. They weren't just lounging around, living aimlessly. They knew what they wanted, and they went after it like there was no tomorrow. I believe in balance. You don't have to push, push, push and never rest. Take it easy when you need to, but that drive should be so alive you'll rest easy on your death bed, grateful that you gave life everything you had.

# LET YOUR SONG RING!

Everyone has a specific purpose, but many people don't know what they want out of life. I've found that with an open mind, trust and seeking, the answers always come. Signs will start popping up. Your heart will start lighting up. Little by little, your path will become clear, and you'll follow your soul.

This has nothing to do with other people or what they think. This has everything to do with you and your journey on a path that you can walk step by step. You will probably need help along the way, but don't let anyone define or direct your path for you. You've got to listen to your soul and figure out the path that best suits you. Often family members pressure us to follow a path that is not true to who we really are. Don't get caught up in that. If what others advise you strikes a cord, by all means, follow it. But don't follow other people's callings. Sometimes I wonder if we forget that life is a precious gift. I wonder if we **real-eyes** that other people are not God. They don't rule us; we don't have to fear them.

Isaiah 2:22 is one of my favorite bible verses: "Stop trusting in mere humans who have but a breath in their nostrils." It's time to trust in something bigger than ourselves. Even if just for the sake of learning not to fear other people. Fearing others seems like a completely irrational thing to me, yet I still sometimes fall victim to it. It's saying, "I'm not going to be myself because I'm afraid of what others will think of me." Who are others to you? I believe that as long as you're not hurting anyone, you can feel free to be yourself.

Set your soul on fire and listen to its desires. Chase after them and be present in every single moment. Talk when you want to talk the way you want to talk. When you stand up for what you believe in, you're the shit because you are doing you! Even if nobody else is rocking with it, keep doing you! Keep your head held high! Do you and be you. Someone will always be hating on you and judging you. There will always be someone who doesn't like you. Fuck 'em! This is about you and the places you wanna go. If they don't support your vision, they can go kick rocks. Someone will always be intimidated by the light you shine. Don't let that get to you.

Someone once told me that if Oprah were to give $1,000,000 to 1,000,000 people, not all of them would like her. Focus on yourself, not what others think. If you feel like dancing and singing, if you feel like saying hello to everyone you meet, do it! If you want to rule the world, work towards that! If you want to be a doctor, be the best doctor you can possibly be. If you want to travel the world, do it twice. Why not? Truly living life means doing you one hundred percent. Stop comparing yourself to others and learn to focus on your own path.

What's the difference between trying to be a better version of yourself and actually *being* a better version of yourself? Nothing. By trying, you are actually doing it. A great therapist used to tell me, "Vanessa, because you are trying, don't think you aren't doing it. You are." And then she would quote Yoda: "There is no try. There is only do." My therapist's point was that by trying to do something, you are actually doing it.

When you are true to yourself, your intuition will lead you on the path that's best for the evolution of your soul. Let your song ring! Let it ring so loudly it drowns out all the other noise. Follow your soul and follow it loyally! Dude, if you want to get tattoos all over your body, by all means, go for it! I recently said fuck it and did my whole back. So long as you're not hurting anyone and you're true to your soul, life is great!

I believe in being as beautiful a person as I can be. To me, being beautiful is having character. It's being a person who genuinely wants to help others when they can. Something very interesting happens when you strive to be a better version of yourself: you begin to be better to others. You treat others the way you treat yourself. In like the saying, "The way you show up to one thing is the way you show up to everything."

Beauty is kindness, but it's not an easy task. Think about how challenging being kind to yourself can be. It's about being kind to others even when you're having a horrible day. It's putting a smile on someone else's face even when you can't seem to put one on yours. It's being loyal. It's not talking badly about others. These are all beautiful characteristics. Think of the characteristics you find beautiful and try to be that way. It's loving who you are and choosing to do what's best for you. Try to live a righteous life. Why on Earth wouldn't you?

# THE ONLY THING THAT CAN STOP YOU IS SELF-DOUBT

We can all try to live our best lives. That means being true to who you are and being the best person, you can be. To be mediocre takes very little effort. I didn't come here to fuck around. I came here to be my best self. I was blessed with legs, arms, a brain, a heart, and so much more. Everyone is talented, everyone has gifts. Everyone has something to give, something to contribute. You owe it to yourself and to the Universe to be your very best. Why be a shitty person when you can be a great one?

It isn't always easy to strive for greatness, but it lies within you. You have it in you to be great. All the greats in history were human beings like you. You deserve to be the best you can be.

Ever notice how easy it is to be mean? Especially if you're paying attention to everything that isn't going right in your life. Being nasty towards others is not a beautiful thing, is it? It's pretty weak. Sure, if somebody pissed you off and you were rude back, it might have felt good for a minute. But deep down, it doesn't feel good to hurt someone. A wise young lady named Rachel Fox once reminded me, "Even unto thyself be harmless." Don't put your dreams aside. Don't beat yourself up. Don't ignore your needs and wishes. Be good to your heart, your soul, and to all the callings within you that truly make you who you are. Honor yourself.

It's important to feel good about who you are. People judge by appearances and live their lives to give a certain impression. I once saw this meme: "God said to love people, not impress them."

A model named Indya Marie inspires me because she stands up proudly for who she is. She posted this caption on one of her photos: "They like me, because I don't need anyone to like me." Have you noticed that when you don't crave attention, most people have a natural liking for you?

When you encounter a situation, you don't like, change it if you can, and if you can't, change your attitude, beliefs, mood. Soon enough, the situation will improve. It's that simple. I met a woman who told me that when she changed her thoughts, her reality changed dramatically and so did she. Her husband said it was like being married to a different person.

It's crazy how capable we all are! Think about the Einstein and Picassos—Marilyn Monroe. I'm sure that they themselves didn't know that they could actualize themselves to those levels, but they did. We all have the ability to do anything we put our minds to. It's a matter of trusting that you can do it. Whether that means trying to be a better person, loving yourself more, creating something or letting go of something. Whatever it may be, you can do it. When you believe in your own ability, your potential is limitless. Focus on what you're made of. Go out there and kick some ass! The only thing that can stop you is self-doubt.

We are human and understand that fear is unavoidable. Just don't let it overcome you. If it does, pick up the pieces, learn, and battle fear again. Keep trying until you get there. Keep going and you'll get what you want or close enough. So long as you keep trying, you're lying to yourself. If you don't try, or you quit without giving yourself a shot, you're not being true to who you truly are. Fear may just be "False Evidence Appearing Real." We usually fear things that haven't happened and never will.

Whenever my friend James tells me he doesn't want to go to the beach because he feels fat, I ask him, "Do you really think people are going to go home and think about you after they leave the beach?" The answer is no! There are tons of people bigger than you, less attractive than you, less intelligent than you."

We live in a world where people wonder, "Will this look okay? Will they think that sounds dumb? Are they going to judge me?" This brings suffering and unhappiness. Dude! You have your one life to live fully and to the best of your ability. Is it worth sacrificing your freedom and truth for the fear of what others may or may not think? Trust yourself. Trust life.

What others think isn't real. How can you know who you really are if you're not true to yourself? This goes for all your inner callings:

your dreams, goals, desires. Choose not to sell yourself short.

Love is the opposite of fear. Love will lead you to follow your soul. Love is the essence of who you really are. It is your true self. I cannot stress this enough. By letting your intuition lead you every step of the way, you'll get where you're trying to go. Sometimes, even if you're clear about your path, you can fall into fear. But by listening to your intuition and letting it guide you step by step, things start to make sense eventually. Dots begin to connect.

# Practices/ Affirmations:
# Be True to You

Repeat this mantra I created to stay in alignment with your soul:

*"May everything I think, say, do and feel be in perfect alignment with my divine purpose and my Higher-Self for my highest good and the highest good of all."*

*"May I honor myself through discipline, compassion and love."*
*Move forward little by little. Before you know it, you will have moved a mountain. Think of the way a building is built and use that as a metaphor. Try to meditate for a few minutes every day. Finish your practice with setting an intention for your day.*
*Use logic when necessary, but follow the callings of your soul. Follow your passions. Trust your soul and trust the Universe.*
*"May I always live according to my Highest Self."*
*"May I practice being my very best self always."*

CHAPTER 7

# Trust

Think back to when you were a child and didn't have a care in the world. Children are totally fearless. Why do you let fear stop you from doing anything? Sometimes, all you need is trust and the belief that things are okay and will be okay. It's hard to just live a life of love, huh. Look at how people handle their lives. Notice how many of us can't handle life well. We become flustered, behave rudely. You can tell by the scrunched up harsh lines on people's faces. So many of us are addicted to pills that ease the "pain." So many of us live in worry, stress, dishonesty, hatred, unhappiness, anger, negativity — all because of fear. The opposite of fear is trust, which is basically a beautiful expression of love. When you live in trust, the qualities you experience throughout the day will be ease, joy, contentment, and peace. Your day goes by smoothly when you live in love and trust that everything will be okay.

# POSITIVE EXPECTATIONS LEAD TO POSITIVE RESULTS

Observe objectively and you'll notice a natural ebb and flow. Think about it. Trust flows through everyone, everywhere, at all times, beneath all the bitterness. It's the flow of life. Just take a look at people in line at the checkout counter, people walking by, the sun rising, night falling. A steady flow goes on. How ignorant is it to live as though you're dying? To live as though a catastrophe is happening? To live as though life is coming to beat you on the head. Some people live as though they're in a state of deprivation, desperation. Why? We aren't here for eternity, so we might as well enjoy the time we have.

Look at what you think about throughout the day. Look at your expectations. Are they usually positive or negative? I'm not saying that everything is perfect, but I do believe that everything is in the right place. I have compassion for people who are suffering, but also believe that everything happens for a reason. Everyone has an expiration date.

There will be tragic moments, but once we learn to get out of our own heads, life is sweet most of the time. Look at how life is working in your favor. You may have days when everything moves smoothly, and good things are happening. That's when you can help others have a wonderful day. Sometimes just a smile will be enough because you're in your flow.

Motivational speaker Bryan Tracy maintains that very successful people habitually have positive expectations, which lead to positive results. Think about it. When you want something to turn out well and believe it will, it usually does. The same goes for the opposite. If you really think something is going to be a disaster, it usually is. Your entire reality is within your mind. Everything you see is outside you, but you interpret it from within. The whole universe is within you.

So, if you're living negatively, thinking negatively, acting in a fear-based manner, ultimately, you'll face the consequence called suffering. Buddha said, "Pain is certain, suffering is optional." When something bad happens to us, or something we think is bad, we cause ourselves to suffer so much. We think of all the terrible reasons why it happened. We beat ourselves up and sulk, feeling like a victim. Your reaction is always your choice. It's all perception. That's all it is. You can choose to be proactive or reactive in any situation. You can choose to consciously respond, or you can be a reactive fool. Straight up. And when something happens that causes you pain, you can choose to learn and grow from it or just suffer.

**Kam-Bridge:** When at three weeks of age, Kamden was given a prognosis of only three months to live, my first thought was that it couldn't be true. My second thought was "How can I go about this in the most positive way possible?" I knew this could break me. I knew that perspective, outlook, positive actions, love and most importantly, trust would keep me going. I had to choose to live every single day believing this was happening for a reason beyond my understanding, that it was for my highest good. I had to trust that life was happening *for* me and not *to* me, that these events weren't happening to cause me harm but for my soul's evolution in some shape or form.

So, I chose to look for the lessons and messages the experience held for me. I chose to find ways to make the best of it. I chose to live for a higher purpose. I chose to live for Kamden. I never wanted to let him down as his mommy. And I chose to live for myself. I knew I hadn't come here as a coward. No, I came here with the courage of a mother-fucking lioness. I did it for the sake of my Higher-Self. I wanted to be an inspiration to myself one day.

Sure, it's great to want to inspire others, but what about inspiring yourself? I believe it's necessary to be an inspiration to yourself first and foremost, then to others. How can you inspire others if you can't even inspire the person you live with twenty-four hours a day, every day?

# SURRENDER TO TRUST

I had to **real-eyes** that life isn't out to get me, that there's a bigger picture than just me. Sometimes really bad things happen, and we may not know why, but that doesn't mean we'll have a bad life. If I chose that perspective, I wouldn't be such a happy camper now, would I? I had tons of suicidal thoughts after Kamden was diagnosed. To be brutally honest, it was hard as fuck, by far the hardest thing I've ever gone through. There's a very dark side to my story, and that's life, right? Just because a hurricane may hit once or twice, doesn't mean you're destined for a doomsday life. Life will get sweet again. Just like it gets dark, it also gets bright, and the light usually lasts much longer than the darkness.

So, shouldn't we all be living fearlessly? If we use logic and really think about things, is it rational to live in fear for the majority of our lives? No. Let's say you're going to meet up with friends and your mind starts racing with irrational thoughts like "OMG! I wonder if they're going to think I'm crazy by saying that?" None of that is happening, so how is that even rational? Is it really worth fearing the prospect of what others will think of you?

The real kicker is that none of this is real. We are all eternal, and in its purest essence, the soul knows that. When we die, our soul goes on. So, is fear something you need to believe in?

Life has brought you this far, hasn't it? If life was so scary, don't you think you would've been gone a long time ago? If all the things we fear really did happen, we'd still be okay, right? People are afraid to fall in love because they're afraid of getting hurt. But if you fell in love and got hurt, you'd still be okay sooner or later. Maybe you're afraid to ask for a raise or a promotion or extra credit in class, scared to speak out, to ask a question.. Maybe you're afraid of change, afraid to move, but even if it didn't work out, you'd survive, right? Dude, if it doesn't kill you, it will make you stronger. Think about the worst things that could ever happen. You might as well think about them since you seem to be doing that subconsciously, anyway. You'd survive, wouldn't you? I hope you **real- eyes** that. You can find relief in knowing that you are an eternal being.

When people lose a loved one, they say "We know she's in a better place now." Or "I know she's watching over me." Which they are. Why are we so afraid? Afraid of being judged, afraid of a car accident, afraid of failing, afraid of looking "small," afraid of not fulfilling all our dreams. We're afraid of all these things because we're afraid of dying. Somewhere in our psyche we fear that if any of these things happen, we'll die.

Buddhist monks practice focusing on their death in order to welcome more joy into their lives. They believe it makes them contemplate if they're making the most of life and the precious short time we have. Try not to be so afraid of life. Surrender to life itself and trust that when you do die, you'll still be fine. You were fine before you got here and you'll be fine when you leave. That thought might be scary, but it's the truth.

Surrender to trusting that everything will work out for your higher good, and that even if it doesn't, you'll still be fine. The question to ask yourself is whether you want to live in fear or in trust. To live in trust means agreeing to live in the present moment. You can only flow in the magic of trust in the now. Living in worry is living in fear of the future. Try it. Even try thinking positive thoughts about the future. Your ego loves to get in the way, and you may begin to fear the future. But beneath the ego is love, and love is trust. To live in trust, you need to let go of the past and the future.

Choose. Choose to trust that your day will be perfect. Trust that even if it is less than perfect, you will handle it to the best of your ability. Trust that every moment is where you need it to be. Trust that things in your life and in the lives of those around you are unfolding perfectly. Trust that you are overcoming your fears. Trust that you are learning how to be the best you can be. Trust that you are capable. Trust that you are confident. Trust that you are worthy. Trust that you deserve the best. Trust that you will have a beautiful life. Trust that you are a good, loving and forgiving person. Trust that you are strong. Trust that you are beautiful. Trust that you are perfect just the way you are. Trust that you will see better days. Trust that what your heart truly desires, you will attain. Trust that you are happy or that you will be happy very soon so long as you keep creating a positive life for yourself. Trust that you are loved. Trust that you approve of yourself. Trust that you don't need anyone's validation. Trust that there is always room for growth. Trust that you are constantly working to improve yourself. Trust that although you willingly opened your heart to someone who crushed it to pieces, you will love again.

Don't give away your power. Don't allow fear to control you. No! You are here to live freely, damnit. Not in a paralyzed, closed off state full of fear. That is not living. That is not life.

You have every right to trust that the universe is working on your behalf. Too often we feel that things are not good enough. Things are not happening as smoothly as they should. Dude, you can live trusting that the best situations and circumstances will materialize. If your intentions are good, and if you trust, you will bring positive results into your life. **Real-eyes** that you live in the universe. An ABUNDANT Universe full of everything that has ever existed. You live on a planet where there are freaking mountains, for crying out loud. There are skyscrapers thousands of feet high. There are geniuses among us who will go invent things that will change the world.

I love a Radiohead video called "Everything in its right place." It shows all types of things the mind might be quick to hear as "wrong," and confirms that things are just as they should be. I believe that everything in my life is just as it should be. This little motto allows me to trust that life is working out the way it's supposed to and it's okay for me to trust it. It's okay for me to trust that the Universe is supporting me. Heck, the Universe supports freaking animals and plants why wouldn't it support me? I just have to believe in it.

A friend recently asked me if I thought I could trust again after a heartbreak. We all want love and a lot of us don't know how to open up to it because we're afraid. After you open your heart to someone who hurts you, it can be scary to get back out there. So sure, I've been scared to love again. My response to her was "Yes, I do think I will trust again." She asked, "How? He hurt you so badly." I said, "My ex is an asshole and I'm still working through healing from that. But I know that I will trust again because I have decided to... I am not going to let an idiot like him ruin my future. Because I trust in the Universe, I know I will trust in love again."

Pause a couple of times a day and state, "Universe, I trust you." See how this shifts your perspective. My ability to trust is in my own hands and in the hands of the Universe. It's a proactive mutual relationship. It's about walking in faith knowing that something much greater is supporting you because you trust it to do so.

Living a life in trust is basically learning to live true to yourself and the callings of your soul. Steve Jobs once said, "Remembering that I'll be dead soon is the most important tool I've ever encountered to help me make the big choices in life. Because almost all fear of embarrassment or failure... these things just fall away in the face of death, leaving only what is truly important. Remembering that you are going to die is the best way I know to avoid the trap of thinking you have something to lose. You are already naked. There is no reason not to follow your heart."

I've learned that's the only way to be happy, to have peace of mind, is to love myself. If I'm not living true to myself, all kinds of confusion is going on inside me. I believe that living a life in trust is about listening to that little voice within you. It's actually a very powerful voice but the tone can be very subtle. It's the little voice that says "Don't go there," or "You know he's not the one," or "I don't know about her intentions," or "Maybe I should be doing something more purposeful with my life." I'm sure you've heard this voice many times. This intuitive voice can lead us to the truth. If you follow it, it can open your heart, bringing you great fulfillment.

Have you ever read a book or watched something on television that might be considered unconventional, something a lot of people would call crazy but rings true to you? That means your heart is speaking. Your heart is the sound of your inner voice, your Higher-Self, your truth. If you listened to your truth and honored it, you would live a life of trust.

And when you live in trust, you attract positivity, so good things start to happen. It's natural to feel fear or doubt about things you want badly. The more you want it, the more you fear not getting it. I don't know why that happens, but I know it does. Think about something you want really badly. Chances are, just the thought of attaining it frightens you. Maybe to the point where that fear gets in your way. You have to choose to rule out that fear. Remove all doubt. Let your belief that you are worthy of having whatever you want be greater than your fear.

I've come to **real-eyes** that most people are afraid of their own power, afraid to shine. Afraid to **real-eyes** that they are good enough. Afraid to receive. For years, I was afraid of my beauty, afraid of my personality. I was afraid I'd make others feel badly by shining in my greatness freely and confidently. Marianne Williamson once said, "There is nothing enlightened about shrinking so that other people won't feel insecure around you." She also said, "Our deepest fear is not that we are inadequate. Our deepest fear is that we are powerful beyond measure."

If this is true, which deep down you know it is, then why not believe it? Deep down within you, you know that you are powerful. So fight your demons with full faith in your soul. The Bible tells us to be confident in spirit and not in flesh. The spirit is infinite and can never die. The Bible says that the flesh is weak, but the spirit is strong. The Bible also tells us to walk according to faith and not sight, meaning that we should trust in the spirit and not in what appears to be real around us.

How many people live in fear? How much sadness do you see around you? Living in a world filled with negativity makes it hard to walk in faith. It's easier to believe negative comments like "That will never happen," "What's wrong with you?" or "How could you believe that would ever work out?"

When you hear these comments, throw up a big internal "Oh yeah? Watch! I'll show you what I'm really made of." Don't let the things people say discourage you. Use them to reaffirm your faith and trust. You are here for a reason. Use the times you feel the lowest as an opportunity to practice living in trust, a chance to prove to yourself that you'll do the damned thing. Trust that anything is possible if you put your mind to it and work hard for it. Trust that you are where you need to be right now for a very specific reason, even if you don't know what that reason is.

Life never ceases to amaze me. I can be at my lowest, feeling all hope is lost and then **real-eyes** I can actually choose faith. I'll get on my knees and say, "Universe, I trust that you will work this out." I've done this numerous times when I've had no clue how I was going to make ends meet, and, somehow, they do. I simply decided to believe they would. I allowed myself to keep moving forward. I didn't just sit on my ass and expect money to fall from the ceiling, but I believed I'd be okay. I chose not to live in fear and to trust that somehow, I'd have enough by the time the rent was due. I didn't waste time worrying. And boom! Somehow, some way, I had enough money to pay the rent. So many times, I've gotten by with some effort, and a lot of faith! (In order to have fight, you've gotta have faith. In order to have faith, you've gotta have fight.)

We don't know what the future will bring. Anything can happen at any time. Sometimes good things happen, and sometimes challenging things. We can't always control it. But we can control how we cope with it. I've lived on faith long enough to believe that the Universe works with you, especially when you believe in it. Even when the odds seem to be against you, if you overrule doubt with trust, things have a way of working themselves out in due time. Sometimes you might have to be a little patient, but that's okay. Put your feet up, sit back and let the Universe figure some of it out for you. You have tomorrow and next month and hopefully, next year. Chill out and stop living in fear.

Believe that you can attain your goals, because the truth is, you can. We are all powerful beings with limitless potential. Deep down, you know this. So, start living in trust. Start giving high fives and hugs to the Creator. Try to have good energy even in the midst of a storm and see how things work. Enjoy the life that was given to you as a gift. Do yourself the favor of trusting that things will work out for the best! Only you have the power to live your life this way. This path is not an easy one. It requires a lot of courage because most of us are ruled by fear. Choose trust. Whisper the word "trust" to yourself often.

# Practices/ Affirmation) to Help You Live in Trust

*Next time you notice you're nervous about something, whisper to yourself "Trust." Make this a habit.*

*Ask yourself to be logical. Is your life really in danger? If not, **real-eyes** it's not logical to be afraid right now. Focus on the fact that life is very short. You are not promised tomorrow. And you only have one life to live. **Real-eyes** that life is too short to be afraid. Practice looking on the bright side of life. It can be very easy to go down the rabbit hole of thoughts that lead to fear. Be mindful of where your thoughts are leading you.*

*Practice trusting your intuition.*

*"I am where I am supposed to be right now."*

*"Everything is unfolding exactly how my soul intended it to unfold for my greater good."*

*"Everything is happening for the evolution of my soul."*

*"I will never leave your side."*

*"Have no fear, God is here."*

*"If you trust Me, you can trust yourself," signed God.*

CHAPTER 8

# Self-Confidence/ Godfidence

Do you believe in yourself? A little bit or a lot? Sometimes or all the time? Do you believe in some of your capabilities or all of them? Do you believe you have what it takes to kill it? Crush it? Do you act with all your power at any given moment? Even when you're going for something you truly desire? Do you believe you can attain anything and that anything is possible? What does belief mean to you? Napoleon Hill said that if a man isn't practicing self-confidence, he's not being confident. He also said, "You can if you believe you can."

My definition of self- confidence is the ability to believe in yourself. Confidence can be measured by how much you practice your belief in yourself. It's having faith in yourself. Everyone has potential, but not everyone has self -confidence. No one can give you confidence. You have to find it yourself. Confidence will make or break you in landing that job, the relationship you really want. Confidence is what allows you to feel comfortable in social settings, to speak openly and publicly, and the list goes on.

You can actively choose to behave self-confidently in any situation. You can be doing something as simple as what I'm doing right now, sitting at a coffee shop, listening to music and typing away, and choose to feel comfortable and confident, or insecure and afraid. Your self-dialogue might become negative. You might tell yourself, "I could never publish anything. They'll all think it's garbage. I'm not going anywhere, anyway." This negative self-dialogue might only last a few seconds, but it could immobilize you. You may not even **real-eyes** it. You might call it writer's block, but in reality, your negative thoughts led you to question yourself and your ability. So, you freeze. You become paralyzed and are unable to perform as a confident person. The choice of your thoughts is always yours.

The same goes for meeting someone for the first time. You can approach the situation with confidence and look the person directly in the eyes, shake their hand and smile, feeling good about yourself. Or you can meet that person feeling completely insecure. Instead of shaking their hand firmly, you can give a weak handshake. Instead of making direct eye contact, you can look down. Instead of smiling, your face might look tense. Your energy will be off.

Self- confidence is energy. Its power. It's a muscle, a shift that switches within you. It says, "I've got what it takes, and I know I've got this!" And you act within that mood. You tell yourself, "I'm gonna show the world what I'm made of." And choose not to let ANYTHING deter you from that belief. Self-confidence is the ability to believe you're hot stuff although your past may not support that idea. It's believing you're smart even if you've been told you're stupid. It's believing you're beautiful after someone you loved treated you like a piece of dirt. It's believing it's perfectly fine to be your weird, unique self. It's never needing the validation of other people, honoring your own opinions and beliefs because they are true for you, holding your head high and never dimming your light.

When you're self-confident, you're so secure within yourself it shows in everything you touch. You know your own capabilities and believe they're definitely more than enough, no matter what others may think. You truly believe you're worthy.

# REWRITE YOUR STORY

Only you can teach yourself to be self-confident. Little by little, with determination and practice, you can build confidence within yourself. Look at it like a muscle. When you use it, it gets stronger. You're still alive and you have room to grow. Look at the way nature is always evolving, always growing. Even with age, we continue to grow. So why sell yourself short? Why not push yourself to be better? You owe it to yourself to believe in yourself, You chose to come here. What sense would it make to think of yourself as a mediocre piece of whatever when, in reality, you're capable of doing anything.

Why do you have low self-esteem? Sometimes in order to fix the problem, you have to go a little deeper and figure out where it began. Sometimes we suffer from low self-esteem because of situations in childhood that made us feel bad about who we are. Someone may have told you that you can't do something... When I was in the sixth grade, I got into performing for our school carnival. I sang in groups with other girls. One year, after we performed Destiny's Child's "No No No," one of the other girls told me I couldn't sing. After that, I only sang freely in the shower when I knew no one else was listening. Only you can teach yourself to be self-confident. I was too young to understand that she was probably just a hater.

It could have been anything. Maybe you were called fat or were abused as a child. At root level, you believe you are unworthy as a human being. You may think it's as simple as a minor case of social anxiety, but it's much deeper.

The key is to go where you may not want to go and challenge those beliefs with change. Changing the way the old you thought, felt, and acted. Your thoughts influence your feelings and you feelings influence your actions. Muster up the courage within to look at things you may not want to see. This might mean facing the fact that you were sexually abused, or something as simple as being told not to look in the mirror, revisiting the experiences that made you feel less than you truly are, and giving love to the part of yourself that was hurting. This is hard to do, but without it, you can't heal. You can rewrite your story. The power lies within you. The great news is you can start rebuilding within yourself at any point you choose. So why wait?

Have you ever seen someone who exudes so much confidence it's intoxicating? Do you think they were born like that? No, they had to work hard. In Napoleon Hill's book, The Law of Success in Sixteen Lessons, published in 1928, was the result of his twenty-year study of the most successful people in the world. He identified sixteen tools they all utilized and dedicated an entire chapter to self-confidence. If you think about it, no successful person lacks self-confidence. Take note of some of your favorite icons, people who have lived before you and use them to inspire you.

There are people who can lift a car with their bare hands, people who build empires. The world keeps evolving and so does human potential. Imagine what the world will be like one hundred years from now, the capacity people will have discovered. Believe in yourself because the truth is you don't know how far you can go. Shit, you just might surprise yourself.

Nothing makes you different from anyone else. The greatest people who ever lived, Benjamin Franklin, Marilyn Monroe, Abraham Lincoln, Dr. Martin Luther King, were not aliens who came to this planet to conquer it. They were normal human beings like you and me. We all have limitless potential, infinite possibilities, and the capacity to create things no one has ever imagined. This is great news! This means that whatever you want to pursue, you can achieve success. But this can only happen if you believe in yourself.

There is no way we were born just to be okay. There is no excuse for not following your dreams, no excuse for not believing in yourself. Yes, it may be hard, but that's never an excuse. You have to want the best for yourself. We are human beings created with higher intelligence. So why wouldn't you do everything possible to achieve everything you want?

If things are hard at times, which they inevitably will be in this gift called life, what are you going to do? Sit there and cry like a baby? Relish in a pity party? It can be healthy to cry at times. It's cathartic and cleansing. Even giving yourself a pity party can be healing. Especially if you limit the limited time and then get off the pity pot and start moving. What I am saying is that you didn't come to this Earth to sit on your ass and feel sorry for yourself. No. We're all strong. We're all built for this life.

**Kam-Bridge:** When I found out about Kamden's diagnosis, as challenging as it was, an innate part of my soul knew I could handle it. If anyone could get through something like that, I knew it was me. I constantly told myself, "God doesn't give anyone anything they can't handle." And through that phrase, I bonded with God who knew me all too well. I'm still here, right? And if I could do it, so can you. You came here to win, whatever winning means for you. You came here to do what they said you couldn't do.

A friend told me that she really wants to write, but when she was a very young child, her parents beat her because of something they read in her journal. I believe she could very well continue writing in her journal and publish it. Who knows what talents she has that need to be unleashed? Our lives unfold according to the thing we came here to fulfill, and it doesn't matter what anyone else says or thinks because it's your life, and you need to care of yourself first. People are far too opinionated.

# YOUR LIFE IS YOURS

# TO LIVE

People will tell you what to do, what not to do, what they think is right, what they think is wrong. They might mean well, but unless you ask for someone's opinion, it might be better left unsaid. Your life is yours to live, not theirs. The Universe will give you the signs you need at the moment you need to receive them. Until you see the signs, just keep doing you. Loud and proud.

At times, I've been afraid I might make someone insecure because I felt good about myself. Was I being loving to myself? No! If I feel good about myself, then damnit, so be it. I posted revealing photos on social media. Maybe I was wearing nothing but lingerie. I was home and I was in that mood. Family members and "friends," called to tell me they had a problem with the photos. I'm sorry, I didn't know I was personally offending you. Last time I checked, I was simply living my life. And my life has nothing to do with you. Whoever you are. You may be in my life but that does not mean you have any say in what I do or how I choose to live. It's my responsibility to make it the best life possible. When I die, whose life will I contemplate?

Which is not to say to be careless about your feelings and sense of entitlement. It's important to understand that others have the right to feel insecure. Their insecurities are not your responsibility and have nothing to do with you. You have enough work to do on yourself. You'll know what that work is, because the same lessons will continuously pop up for you. Life is like a school with lessons, tests, and chances to try again. Sometimes you fail sometimes you pass, other times you reflect. The point is that you know you're here to work hard on yourself; within yourself. I'm talking about building yourself up so you can have the life you want and deserve, so you can be the best version of yourself. And to do that requires an immense belief in yourself.

You can't build self-confidence without wanting it very badly. Anything you achieve takes hard work, the belief that you can attain what you're going after, and first and foremost, the desire to attain it. We all struggle with insecurities. Maybe you didn't pass an audition because you weren't good enough to make the cut. Maybe you see the girl of your dreams every day, but you can't find the confidence to approach her. You're good enough, so long as you believe you are.

You are just as worthy as anyone else. What would make someone better than you? The money they have? The job they landed? The clothes they wear? None of these *things* mean that person is better than you. If you believe that person is better than you, then you're putting down your own self-worth. They have those things not because they're better than you but because they believed that they were capable of attaining them.

Never compare yourself to others because you are a unique individual. Ask yourself if you'd really like to be like someone else. Do you want the hand they were dealt? All the cards, not just the aces. I don't want anyone else's life. I want to be my genuine self, and I'm happy with who I am. I don't want anybody else's problems, and no matter how green the grass may look on their side of the fence, believe me, they have problems just like you do.

The easiest way to destroy your self-esteem is by wishing you were someone else or had what they had. Comparing yourself to others will destroy your soul and your belief in your own greatness. It will cause you to compete (even subconsciously) when the only competition is with yourself. What would you win at the end of your made-up competition? You're not competing so you can be better than anyone else. You're competing to be the best you can be. And you can't be your best self when you're focused on someone else. So, don't ever get into the destructive habit of comparing yourself to others. Stop if you notice it and ask yourself if you would really want their life.

Comparison can only be healthy if it inspires you. Just as Barak Obama could become the first Black president of the United States, if you put forth the work and believe in yourself, you can achieve your own goals. With dedication, time, *faith* and persistence. Who knows what you're capable of?

Have you ever walked into a job interview or a contest or anything you wanted to be chosen for really badly and told yourself that you knew you'd get it? If you didn't have even the slightest inkling of doubt and you brought your A-game, what happened? I'll bet you got it. Think back to anything you've achieved that you really wanted. You achieved it because you believed you could.

A psychotherapist once told me that everyone is insecure, but we each have our own way of covering it up. I want a soul brave enough to unmask those insecurities, to come clean and admit who they are. Why cover up with excessive makeup, flashy name brands, showing off? You know what I'm talking about, the things we feel we have to do to prove our worth to others. Just be you and believe that you're good enough.

If you like name brands, there's nothing wrong with that. There's nothing wrong with admitting how good you feel about yourself from time to time. You'll get haters, but fuck 'em. Do what you love and what makes you happy. Just don't live to impress other people.

I recently had a conversation with someone about the mask of "self-confidence" some people wear versus true self-confidence, which stems from within. For instance, just because someone looks like they think they're the shit in a photograph, doesn't mean they truly believe it. They may be very vain or cunning enough to know how to put on that poker face. But a truly confident person doesn't have to "put on" or "try too hard," to let others know that they believe in themselves.

A truly confident person is comfortable simply being themselves. There's nothing to prove, no attention to be received, and no one to convince that they're good enough. You can spot these people instantly by noticing that they *really* don't care about what others think about them. They usually don't follow the current trend, and they're not afraid of others. You can see it in their behavior. They may almost seem careless because they truly don't care what others think of them. They are just being themselves.

I'm still working on this one, and I'm proud to say that I'm beginning to see improvements. I spend a lot of time in crowded coffee shops, and if hip-hop is playing in the background, I'll bop my head to the rhythm. And guess what? I don't give a fuck what anyone thinks. I feel liberated within my soul, and this confidence is becoming so much a part of my essence it carries over to the way I move.

The way I get up from a chair, my walk, what I'm thinking or feeling, reflect supreme confidence. It's almost like I step into a higher part of myself. the part that's aware of my full potential. I go down the rabbit hole to the place where I find all my strengths and accomplishments, the place that leads me to an aspect of myself, I never knew existed, where I can love on some Vanessa. When I'm in the mood, I say to myself "Vee, I Love Thee." It took me a while to get where I am now and I'm still working on it.

I **real-eyes-ed** that true self-confidence comes from first recognizing your attachment to the approval of others. We all subconsciously search for this because we all need love. We've all experienced lack of love at one point or another. It could have been something as extreme as abandonment by your parents or something as simple as a childhood friend having to cancel on you. It could be that your teacher told you to wash your book bag, and you still think of yourself as "dirty," not good enough to be accepted by others. The truth is that we're all sensitive beings and we all need love. We're never taught how to love ourselves enough, so we search for that love in others.

We want validation from others more than ever before because of the times we're living in. With social media, we constantly see altered images of people living lies, and consciously or not, we compare ourselves to those unnatural ideals. We're living in a time when images, likes and comments make a huge difference in our lives and the way we feel about ourselves. This makes us seek validation from others. It teaches us that we're no longer good enough. We're only as good as other people think we are, and we look to them for love, approval, and validation, instead of looking within ourselves.

It's almost as though we place the power that lies within us in the hands of others, because we care so much about what they think.

# CHOOSE TO ACCEPT YOUR AUTHENTIC SELF

The key is to love yourself so much that it doesn't matter whether people like you. Not everyone will like you, no matter how great you are. No matter how much success you achieve, you may be brutally attacked by hatred. So, choose not to live for others. Choose not to be afraid of how you may appear. Choose to accept your authentic self exactly as you are.

Who cares if they don't accept you?! Can they live your life for you? Do they have to face you on your death bed? NO! Only you can ask yourself if you're truly satisfied with how you lived your life! Live for yourself and for what feels right to you. Be true to yourself. Don't lie to yourself. Your power and your love lie within you and neither of these can be found outside yourself. It's all a part of your journey, all part of your path, all part of loving yourself.

You were born as love, then brought into a society where self-love is not taught. You need to discover how to love yourself for who you truly are. Learning to love yourself is beautiful. We get to rediscover and recreate ourselves, to grow. What better way to express love than through evolution? I think it has something to do with our purpose in life and why we're truly here. We're all able to be compassionate with ourselves and others, but you can't really love anyone if you don't love yourself first. The more you love your life, the more you'll love yourself and vice versa.

When I was in high school, I saw a short film, definitely a B movie, but I found it interesting. In the film, we all begin as souls doing nothing but meditating or praying. One by one, we each get a turn to go into the room to watch what our lives will be like in the future. One soul sees herself as a little girl with both parents. When she's five years-old, her dad dies. She's sad but has beautiful memories. She goes to high school, college, gets married and has a daughter. When her daughter is eleven-years-old, she hears her calling for her in the living room. When she gets there, she sees that her daughter has fallen and been injured. The daughter is paralyzed for the rest of her life. The film shows the sad woman pushing her daughter around in a wheelchair. She goes to the "big boss" (a.k.a. God,) who is sitting in his office showing her all this and tells him, "No! I don't want to be born. I don't want to suffer all that pain." She runs out of the office and goes back to being a soul meditating with all the other souls. But then she thinks about it and returns to the boss's office. "I changed my mind," she says. "I want to be born. I want to feel joy, pain, laughter, good experiences! I want to experience everything."

Think about your life objectively for a moment. View it from an objective perspective. The way your life has turned out thus far hasn't been that bad, has it? Take in all the ways it has shaped you into the person you are today. Would you really have wanted things to be so different? Think about the way you dress, the way you talk, the beautiful experiences you've had, and the bad. The neighborhood you grew up in. The family you were blessed with. The music you grew to love and why.

A line in one of Future's songs goes "The good, the bad and the ugly, you can't let none of that shit get to you, man." And that's real. If we all come here by choice, then isn't it something we wanted for our lives?

**Kam-bridge:** When Kamden was in the NICU, before anyone knew what was wrong with him, a pediatrician told me that my son had chosen me. Maybe he knew the kind of loving I would give him. Maybe his soul came here to get loved on. Maybe he came here just for love. And he chose me because he knew I would be capable of loving him unconditionally with my whole heart. Our souls come here for a much higher purposes than we can understand. So, fuck people's thoughts about you. Do you. And do it with love. Self-love is self-confidence.

Put the need for validation away. The hell with it. Validate yourself. You're cool because you say you're cool. Screw what others think is cool. Be the individual you were created to be. Let go of the need to compete with others; of constantly needing to prove yourself. Life is not about seeing who the best is. There *is* no best.

We're here to be the best versions of ourselves. Because really, no one is better than anyone else. And whatever "best" means to you is all that matters. You don't have to live up to anyone else's standards. I found this quote on Instagram: "If the world was blind, how many people would you impress?" Who are you living for? Whose acceptance are you striving for? It all lies within your, or it should, because no one can truly validate you but yourself and God.

Learn to stand up for yourself. Standing up for your beliefs is a sign of self-love. You might have to tell people not to fuck with you. A self-confident person knows how to stand up for what they believe in. They know how to love on their souls. They know how to believe in all they are capable of achieving. It's about coming from your soul, the core of your gut, and constantly striving to be better because you know you can.

You're a divine being who is only here for a quick round, so might as well give it your best shot, all the while striving to go deeper, looking for more love within yourself. This journey does not end. There is no ending point when you say, "That's it. I've made it. There's nothing left for me to learn, nowhere for me to grow. No better version of myself to discover."

Life is love. Love is infinite. There's so much more room for love on this journey.

# Practices/Affirmations to Help You Believe in You

*Whenever you compare yourself to others, gently say, "No, we're not gonna go there. I'm gonna stay in my lane and keep living my life."*

*Listen to music and use it to feel good about yourself. Something with soul. A really great one when you feel like celebrating how far you have come is "Private Party" by India Arie. But rap, rock & roll, whatever moves your soul. Jump up and get crazy with yourself.*

*Focus on the good things about you. On your strengths. Your accomplishments. The things that make you unique.*

*"I am worthy of believing in me."*

*If I don't believe in me, who will? Believe, even if it's all you've got.*

*"I am worth it."*

*"I am good enough."*

*"My mind is strong, and I believe in mind over matter."*

*"I can do anything I put my mind to."*

CHAPTER 9

# Forgiveness

*If you do not forgive men their sins, your
Father will not forgive you your sins.*

**Matthew 6:14.**

It makes no difference what your religious beliefs or practices are. We're all going to the same place, the same Source energy from which we all derive. It's simply a matter of the path you choose. I love the Quran, the Bhagavad Gita, Upanishads — any ancient text filled with sacred wisdom. You can find gems in all of them. The quote I've chosen from the New Testament makes a valid point: How can you ask to be forgiven if can't forgive others?

We're all one and it's important that we're taking this journey collectively. We all make mistakes. No one is ever perfect. I have **real-eyes-ed** that when others hurt us, intentionally or unintentionally, it's not personal. They hurt others because they themselves are hurt! Their cup is overflowing with hurt and spills onto others.

I had an associate who was very envious and had what I perceived as ill intentions. Was it my fault? No, because I was simply being myself. Was it her fault? No, because I **real-eyes-ed** she had a lot of insecurities and placed them on me, most likely unintentionally. She felt so badly about herself and who she was that she began to hate me for everything she was not.

At the time, I felt it was personal, but truly, it was not. It's not my fault if someone chooses to compare themselves to me. Everyone has a choice to compare themselves to others or not. I personally choose not to — ever. No comparison can ever be real, because we are each unique. Just as no two snowflakes are exactly alike, no two people are identical. So why waste your time? Comparison only brings misery. Have you noticed?

Comparison makes you feel badly about yourself, less than the other. Ever hang out with someone and wonder why you felt bad about yourself the whole time? The other person probably didn't do or say anything to make you feel that way, yet you felt inadequate because you were unconsciously comparing yourself and deciding you were less worthy, based entirely on your own opinion of the other person's value. It's not healthy and it's not real.

Let's say what you're doing is not so much comparing yourself but hyper-focusing on someone's qualities. It's very easy to feel badly and you wish you had what the other person has, even if you're simply admiring them as inspiration. The line between inspiration and envy is very fine. The person may inspire you so much you may unconsciously begin to emulate them. That only takes you farther from yourself. Your insecurities may begin to manifest in ugly ways. We often think someone is being nasty, but what's really happening is their insecurities are getting the best of them.

When I was working as a waitress, I served a guest who went in for the kill the moment she saw me. I was taken aback. I'd simply asked which wine she preferred. She was very condescending and long story short, called me a bitch. I told her, "Do not fuck with me." The interesting thing is that her insecurities came up. When it was time for her to pay, I didn't acknowledge her presence. She blurted out, "What? You think I don't have any credit cards to pay for this? I can pay for this!" Mind you, it was St. Patrick's Day, so she may have been plastered. But when did I insinuate that she may not have been able to pay? A person's insecurities always reveal themselves eventually.

When you encounter someone who hates themselves that much, try to have compassion for them and where they are on their journey. Keep it moving with your peaceful and loving self. Send them good vibes, then do yourself a favor and get away from that toxic energy. You can always send light and love vibrations from a distance.

# RELEASE BAD ENERGY

People sometimes go through storms. You can try to be understanding without letting others treat you badly. Have you heard the saying "Forgive them not for them, but for your own peace of mind"? When you don't forgive someone, you become bitter and closed off, and your pain lasts much longer than it should, because the grudge is stuck inside you. The hurt already came and went, so why stay mad about it? We think, "This and that happened in the past, so it will happen again." Or we let thoughts of the past consume our lives, leaving us angry or bitter. This may be unconscious, but the anger will permeate our lives in surprising ways. It might appear when you least expect it, and you'll blow up over something minor. **Real-eyes** that the incident is long gone!

Let's say you date someone and they do you wrong. When you meet a new person, you treat them as though they're your ex. You a have your guns up, expecting to be hurt again. This is irrational. This person hasn't hurt you, and they may never hurt you, but your defenses are up because you haven't healed from the past.

We all want to be at peace. This goes for any situation we have not forgiven. Let's say you were involved in a traumatic car accident that left you paralyzed with fear, and you chose never to drive again. Some people live their lives in a constant state of resentment or fear.

Because you can't forgive or heal, you suffer, but the person who did you wrong isn't moved the slightest bit. They're most likely getting on with their life oblivious to your feelings. So, it's important to take care of yourself. Self-care is the best care. WWhen you choose not to forgive, that grudge remains within you, and whenever something reminds you of the perceived wrong, you get tense and angry. Every time you hear the name of the person who did you wrong, a chemical reaction goes off in your body. Even if you think you've forgiven the person, you may become aware of a physical reaction. You may grind your teeth or clench your hands. Pay attention to the way you feel about the person or situation. Forgiving is a process. Sometimes it's a whole fucking journey!

We may want to forgive as quickly as possible, especially if it's something that really pissed us off, because we want the pain to go away. But that's usually when it takes the most time and effort. We may say to ourselves, "I'm over that. I forgave her." But it's usually a very deep repetitive process that requires a lot of introspection.

Forgiveness is a matter of the heart. It requires a lot of courage. Look at the person who hurt you. Then transmute that pain. Release the person and the act that hurt you so badly. Until you can do this, you are that person's prisoner. A powerful coach once taught me to do mirror work around forgiveness. It goes like this: Stand in front of a mirror looking right into your eyes and call the person who hurt you. Say their name while looking right in the mirror and express everything you feel about the situation. This is an effective method for releasing bad energy. You can move your hands after your statement to further transmute this energy and confirm that it's been released.

I have found success with releasing resentment through meditation. I compassionately look at what is hurting me and choose to release the pain into the earth so it can be recycled into healthy fertilizer. The earth can bear anything we choose to release. It has its own intelligence system. But we must take those courageous first steps of looking at the hurt, having compassion for the person who caused it, and most importantly, having compassion for ourselves.

If the pain was deep, you won't easily brush it off your shoulders, but if you make forgiveness an everyday part of your life, you can cultivate it like a habit, and it will become easier and easier to forgive. Another very helpful exercise is to **real-eyes** that the person is doing the best they can with what they know how to do. Each of us is on our own journey and a lot of times we're not conscious of the impact our words and actions have on others. We may even think we're doing what's best for them. It's always about intention.

Another perspective that really helps me is believing that the person who hurt me will have to face himself after this life. One day the truth will come out, and he'll have to be accountable for his actions. This has nothing to do with you, but with the evolution of the person's soul and what lessons they need to learn on this journey or the next.

To be capable of forgiving everyone and everything takes a heightened perspective. None of this is easy, but it's worth the fight, because it will help you get through life's challenges. You deserve to be happy and loved. You deserve to live your life in love. The more you come to forgiveness, the more you come to love. It takes a lot of love to forgive.

I love this quote from Saint Francis of Assisi: "Be always patient and well disposed, if one of your brothers offends you in any way, offer to God the pain you experience. By this mark I shall know if you are the true servant of our Divine Master. If you bring back sweetly to God, the brother who has wandered from Him, and if you still continue to love one who has rendered himself very guilty."

The key is having more love. Even when you find it hard to love, love anyway. There can never be enough love because love is infinite. The more love you incorporate into your life, the higher your vibration becomes. The more love you give, the more light will fill you. Who doesn't want good energy? Who doesn't wanna be on that positive wavelength? Spread out those good vibrations. No matter what the crime was.

When you learn to practice forgiveness, life becomes sweeter, and you have less hatred, regret, and resentment — all negative feelings you wouldn't want anyway. Life is just too short for that. Find things greater than yourself to care about, like people in need. Be a little more carefree. Have a little more love in your heart, a little more compassion. When someone betrays you, they teach you not to trust their loyalty. In *The Four Agreements*, Don Miguel Ruiz's Four Agreements, tells us to agree not to take anything personally and understand that the way people treat us is about *them*. If someone hurts you, it's a reflection of who they are, and may have nothing to do with you. Instead of holding a grudge, be grateful that you learned something about that person and decide not to trust them as much as you did before. Thank the Universe for revealing this truth to you sooner than later.

Understand that no one is perfect, and a lot of times people mess up without knowing what they're doing. So, try to let it go. Try to move on with your life as happily as possible because you owe it to yourself. Let go of anger, resentment, and bitterness. You don't deserve to alter yourself or your life because of what someone did to you. You deserve a happy life. And that depends on you, not on someone else.

# YOU ARE THE MOST IMPORTANT PERSON IN YOUR LIFE

Focus on you and creating the best for yourself. Once, I was complaining to this guy that my boyfriend broke up with me, etc. and he was like, "Well the most important thing is you, because no one else is going to take care of you the way you should be taken care of." That was one of the realest things I'd heard in a minute. Truth is that people will do you wrong. They will piss you off. They may hurt your feelings really badly.

YYou won't be able to avoid hurting others if you don't take very good care of yourself. Ever notice how those who hurt us the most probably weren't in the best place? They may be very depressed or constantly disappointed. You may have even noticed that they compare themselves to others often. They may even compare themselves to you. That's a sign of misery.

A close friend complimented me over and over on my strength while I was going through a difficult time. At a certain point, she started going out of her way to share upsetting news with me. Then she began to flip all of her praise to hateful messages about a negative experience in my past. I immediately **real-eyes-ed** she was hurting. She was envious of the fact that I was strong, and she wanted to see me falter. Maybe she thought I had so much of what she wanted for herself that she forgot to see her own light.

People who try to bring you down are not happy with themselves. If they were, they'd be able to admire your achievements without losing sight of their own greatness. They'd know someone else's admirable qualities don't take away their own.

Each one of us has unique qualities. If you see qualities in someone else that you'd like to have, let that be an inspiration, instead of a cause for envy. Each of us has our greatness. I don't care who you are or what you may have done in the past. We are all made of God's essence. Know Thyself.

# SET YOUR INTENTIONS

Life is a classroom. Those of us who focus on the dark side are unaware of our own greatness. They're not taking good care of themselves. I know because I've been there myself. They're usually unaware of their intentions. One way to cultivate a life you truly enjoy is to set intentions throughout the day. People who are caught up in their own misery might not be able to see the importance of setting good intentions. They might not be trying to find happiness within themselves. They might not even be close to taking care of themselves or learning how to put themselves first. Only if you truly love yourself can you love others. You can only give what you have. And in order to give you must be able to receive. Life is an exchange of love, whether through service to your family and loved ones or everyday interactions. Love is who you are, so why wouldn't you want to live in unconditional love and do everything possible to love as unconditionally as possible?

I read an anonymous quote (I sometimes think those are better,) stating, "Your heart has loved you from the beginning." It has! Do you think if you didn't truly love yourself, you'd be here right now? Do you think you would've signed up for this life? Learn to cultivate the love that resides within you. Too many people don't love themselves enough. I've been one of them. And I'm not sure that I'm currently loving myself as much as I should.

There's no limit. There will always be room to love yourself more love and to give more love to others. Try not to be like those miserable people who hate others and feel there's nothing worth loving in life, people who'd rather focus on what's wrong with others than what's right with them. It's as simple as looking for all the beauty around you or finding beauty in the hard lessons we sometimes have to learn. It may be having the courage to find compassion for someone who was so troubled that they hurt you, or in learning to find compassion for yourself.

# CHOOSE COMPASSION. CHOOSE LOVE.

I will never forget listening to "Seat of the Soul," by Gary Zukav. Both Oprah and Maya Angelou swore this book changed their lives for the better. Zukav says that you cannot repay evil with evil, because that will only turn into the same thing. Instead, shed light upon evil because evil doings are simply the absence of light. Have compassion rather than hatred towards evil. Since I've been practicing this way of living, I've felt freer.

An ex- boyfriend wrote me a not so nice email stating, "...and I don't even care about you." Did that hurt? Heck yes. But I shed light onto that situation by replying kindly yet honestly that "It's okay if you don't care about me." Because it *is* okay. I care about myself enough, so I don't need anyone else to care about me. I ended my response with "Take care. Love, Vanessa." If I'd replied with hatred, I would have started a ping pong full of negativity going back and forth. And as Zukov, wrote, it would have reduced me to that same evil he'd chosen. I chose compassion instead.

Try to choose love. You know how ballsy that is? It's always easier to get angry right back. But choose to rise above it and respond with the highest frequency, which is love. Love is the opposite of anger. I understood that he might be angry for whatever reasons, and I chose not to take his words personally. Everyone enters your life to teach you something. We're all in a big campus called "The Journey." Life goes on, with you or without you.

What's the point of taking revenge? Gratification? How long will that last? And how will it affect your karma? What's the point in holding onto anger, anyway? Is there a point? Is the person worth discombobulating your energy? These are questions to ask yourself. Sure, sometimes you may feel entitled to be angry. We all have the right to feel what we feel. But once you feel that anger, dude, let that shit go. Ask yourself, "How is this anger serving me?" or "Is being angry going to help me in any way?" The answer will always be NO.

Anger is not an emotion that can go away in an instant like happiness. Right? We can be happy one second, then someone does something to piss us off — and poof! It's gone. Anger works differently. When you're angry about something, depending on how bad that something made you feel, it can take time to get over it. We're sensitive humans who can't change from angry to happy at the snap of a finger. It's okay if your anger doesn't go away in an instant. But acknowledge that you've decided to choose to let go of that negative frequency so you can raise your vibration and live with inner peace. Choose to move forward with your life and don't let anger control you. No matter how long it takes or how hard it is, persevere and choose forgiveness and happiness. The shit already happened. Why live today stressing over yesterday's disappointments? Yesterday is gone, love. And sometimes, that's a good thing.

It's as easy as repeatedly making a conscious choice to let the anger go. It's deciding to take your power back. Choosing not to give your power to any entity. If you're angry about what Shavonda did to you the other day, that anger controls you. It's standing in the way of your freedom. You're giving your power to Shavonda and what she did. On the other hand, if you center yourself and take power over your own life, you can choose to forgive Shavonda, not for her sake but for your own peace of mind. You can go on living freely and happily without being disturbed by what someone did to you.

If someone did you wrong, it's not your problem. It's not personal. They did that to you because they were fucked up and not in a good place. It's never about you. You may choose to forgive Shavonda because you have compassion and understand that sometimes people make mistakes. None of us are perfect. Everyone is on their own journey doing the best they can. When you forgive in this understanding way, you are not sparing them, you are sparing yourself the burden of pain. Move on to the next moment. Who wants to stay in what bothered them for a long time?

Look at dogs. They get depressed or angry, and a moment later, when they're fed or their owner comes home from a long day at work, they're happy. They never dwell on whatever it was that pissed them off. They know how to live in the now. It makes me believe it's unnatural to hold on to anger. It's natural to get angry, but let that shit go, dude. That energy and negative frequency can't help you be happy. You can't be angry and happy at the same time. You owe it to yourself to be free from pain. To be free from whatever pissed you off yesterday, the day before, the month before and the years before.

Most of us could spend a lifetime forgiving things from our past. But why should it take that long? Life goes on with you or without you, so you might as well move on fully. Why allow yourself to be burdened by things that held you back in the past? Choose a new way to live. Whether it's forgiving your past or your present situation, it starts with you. Making a conscious choice to forgive is a deep process of self-love. You have to go to that tender part deep within your heart that feels the brutal pain of what happened.

# You are your own parent

Often, it's a process of reclaiming your inner child — or your inner adult — from a time when you felt hurt. People who make this conscious, usually painful choice, don't do so because it feels like an ice cream cake on a hot summer day. No, they do it because they love themselves enough to know that they deserve happiness and a new life. They make the choice to forgive, not because it's easy, but because it frees the soul. Another layer of forgiveness goes very deep, to the place where you **real-eyes** you can forgive others because you have forgiven yourself.

We can be so harsh with ourselves, so hurtful to ourselves without **real-eyes-ing** that we need to make a conscious choice to be compassionate with ourselves. The other night I made a mistake at my job, and, boy, did I beat myself up! I was so mad at myself for not being perfect. This made me **real-eyes** that I had to stop and apologize to myself for being so mean to me, for putting up with the harsh critic in my head who constantly demands perfection. It was time for me to take the role of an adult, and to control that inner critic when it wants to come out. It's time I have compassion to really take the wheel of my life. To demand a life free of self-hatred.

Perfectionism is a disease, and it doesn't only show in blatant, obvious mistakes. I began to **real-eyes** that I was cruel to myself and competitive with myself. Once I stopped believing in competing with others, I could only compete with myself. If someone says "You need to do your work much faster" then my mentality will be "Oh yeah? You don't think I can do it? Just watch me!" This could be brutal to my spirit. I have nothing to prove to anyone. I don't have to step up to the plate every time someone says I should improve in some way. I can take the criticism in a positive manner and use it to my benefit. I mean, jeez, it's self-abusive.

Why wouldn't you want to have kind and loving thoughts about yourself on a regular basis? Can you imagine hearing a mother tell her daughter "You're ugly. You're not special. He won't like you back. You don't know how to look pretty like those girls that you see on Instagram. You need to put on all the makeup and all the weave to look halfway decent. You have to drive an expensive car to look like you're something." How are those thoughts being loving to yourself? How are they validating your worth?

Those thoughts are acts of self-hatred. **Real-eyes** that your thoughts and beliefs about yourself are powerful. As Napoleon Hill wrote, "Thoughts are things." Be very careful how you speak to yourself, because self-talk is the basis for self-love or self-hatred. Your thoughts become beliefs, which lead to the way you treat yourself and feel about yourself.

For the longest time, people would rant and rave about how attractive I was. I could never see it. They said it, but I didn't believe it. I hated it because I related my appearance to my history of being sexually abused. But who did that affect? Me or them? Me, of course, because it *is* me. It makes no difference if the whole world perceives me as something admirable, if I don't perceive myself that way or if I associate their compliments with something negative, I'm the one who suffers. We are responsible for our perspectives.

If you want to view yourself as ugly, unworthy, helpless, shitty, be my guest. But **real-eyes** that you can choose what you believe about yourself. You may or may not be flattered by what other people tell you. What's most important is what you believe about yourself. There will always be someone who loves you, and there will always be someone who hates or envies you. Stay in your lane and don't be consumed by other people's opinions of you. Focus on liking yourself. What matters is how you treat you. What matters is the love and care you give yourself. **Real-eyes** that you can choose how you talk to yourself and treat yourself. You can choose to forgive yourself or not. You can choose how you relate to yourself, which inevitably determines how you relate to others. The way you treat yourself will always be a clear reflection of the way you treat others.

You can choose to live comfortably with who you are and freely allow yourself to simply be. Focus on you first so you can be great to others. Be great to yourself, respect yourself. First and foremost, love yourself, nurture yourself. Begin by forgiving yourself. Accept that you haven't always been nice to yourself and try to practice being kind, instead. This may be strange territory for you. That's perfectly fine. You'll find your way little by little.

# FORGIVE YOURSELF

Forgiving yourself is difficult, but it's an important process, because if you don't, you're doomed to be miserable, and the guilt you carry will prevent you from being all you can be. You may be plagued with a feeling of unworthiness that will deprive you of happiness. You will never be able to see others with eyes of love, light and acceptance if you don't see yourself that way. How you feel about others is a projection of the way you feel about yourself.

When was the last time you looked, really looked, at your true essence? Forgiving yourself means accepting yourself, having compassion for yourself at the deepest level. Once you can do that, you can forgive others. How can you expect to have a beautiful future or believe you deserve a beautiful life if you can't forgive yourself to your core?

I recently **real-eyes-ed** that I had to forgive myself for how badly I treated my mother growing up. Sure, I changed over the years and began to treat her much better, but no matter how I treated her, she continued to give me the limitless, unconditional love I'm beyond blessed to receive. As I got older, my biggest fear was that I wouldn't **real-eyes** that I deserved her unconditional love, because I felt undeserving of her goodness. This harbored guilt resulted in a lack of feeling worthy overall, especially since I came into this world through her. There are deep ties there. Because of this, I allowed myself to carry a deep sense of unworthiness. Until I finally told myself, "No. No more feeling like I don't deserve my mother's love, or anyone else's love for that matter. I do deserve love and I do deserve a good, beautiful future."

In order to truly believe this, I had to go to that scary place within myself. I **real-eyes-ed** that if I wanted to stop fearing the guilt, I would have to liberate myself so that I could go where I hadn't been since I was a kid. I had to say to myself, "I understand why you did what you did. I understand why you felt the way you felt. I understand why it was so hard for you to forgive yourself for what you did and the way you treated her. She really is the sweetest soul. I understand you may not have known how to show her your appreciation. I understand that you made mistakes. I understand that this is all okay and that you deserve to forgive yourself. You deserve your love and the love of others. You are worthy, no matter your past. You are worthy, my innocent little Nessa. I understand you."

I once saw a short video in which a professor takes out a dollar bill and asks the class who wants it. Of course, they all raise their hands. Then he crumbles it into a ball and again asks who wants it. Again, everyone raises their hands. Then he throws it on the floor, stomps on it and rubs his shoe into it. Again, he asks who wants the dollar bill, and again, everyone raises their hands. Then he tells the class that this was a very important lesson. Nothing that has happened in your past, diminishes your value. just as the crumpled and dirty bill was still worth a dollar. No matter what you have gone through, you are still and always will be worthy, because you are a living soul with infinite value. You are a divine being. This may be hard to grasp, but it's true.

I recently had to go deep within myself to forgive myself for the way I treated a puppy. When I got her, I was kind to her but not always. I was trying to figure out how to get her house broken. She was a tiny little teacup, and I yelled at her every now and then or tapped her lightly. I don't care how lightly or how seldomly I tapped her. Wrong is wrong. I later **real-eyes-ed** I hadn't treated her as well as I should have. She didn't deserve to be yelled at. Dogs have feelings. We mustn't forget that we're animals, too. She was totally dependent on me. Dogs have no words, but they are loving beings who only mean well. I could have used discipline strategies.

Years later, the thought that I had treated her poorly still haunted me. I only had her for eight months and she was always loving to me. Dogs are unconditional in their love, but we humans attach plenty of conditions to ours. Little by little I did deep self-talks, telling myself, "It's okay. I forgive you." I went deep within and looked at parts of myself I really didn't want to see. I was fortunate enough to go so deep that I envisioned her accepting my forgiveness and receiving me with open arms, licking me all over. At the moment when I envisioned her, I felt free of the guilt. I knew I had released it. I had learned my lesson and I would never treat a living being that way again.

Eventually, I stopped eating meat because I became so connected with the souls of animals. No one and no animal deserves to be yelled at for making an unknowing mistake. This liberated me in such a way that I felt like I could forgive myself and others for anything. But I regularly have reminded myself.

If I can't forgive myself, how can I forgive others? If I can't forgive, how can I be happy? If I fill a dark hole with grudges and animosity towards others or myself, how can I find room or happiness? When you forgive others, you forgive yourself. And you do so through compassion. Why wouldn't you be compassionate towards others and yourself? We are all placed on this Earth without an instruction book. We're not perfect beings and we don't have it all figured out. We're each on a unique journey, a continuous learning process.

A lot of us are broken and trying to find our way to happiness. Sometimes we are hurt by events along the path, and it can be hard for a person who doesn't have all the answers. The hurt causes them to be hurtful in return. I'm not saying that's an excuse, I'm saying it's a reason to be compassionate. Plenty of journeys are hard to walk. **Real-eyes** this and give love. Send light to others. Cultivate reverence.

Tread lightly. Give others the benefit of the doubt. They usually don't know any better and they're doing the best they can. Maybe they're so broken they don't know how to take good care of themselves, so how in the world can they take good care of you?

Alan told me something very wise. He told me to smile more and that no one can ever smile too much. A hater had made fun of how much I smile by mocking me, asking if I smiled 24/7. Alan was saying the opposite, suggesting that everyone should smile as much as possible. He said that life is too short. Just let things go. He's so right. Every single thing you see is temporary. If this moment can never come back, you might as well let it go. Easier said than done, but take note of the wisdom that lies within this truth. Everything is temporary. Ask yourself why you haven't forgiven yourself or someone else.

Choose to take it easy with yourself. You know you're doing the best you can. So, live lightly and forgive yourself frequently. Learn, yes do learn, but most importantly, love. Love yourself enough to be compassionate and understanding with yourself, knowing that you are not perfect and that that is A.O.K. Do the same with others. All of us are imperfect. All of us are at unique places in our journeys.

# Practices/Affirmations
# to Help you Forgive

*Take the time to understand that if someone has hurt you, they're probably hurting themselves and it has nothing to do with you. I'm not suggesting that you forget what they said or did. Instead, have compassion. Understand that they are having a hard time in their journey and need help.*

*Let go of the anger, the hurt, the pain of the past. Even if you have to let it go over and over again. Let go so you can be free. It's a kind of surrender. When thoughts of that person or event enter your mind, tell yourself, "I'm choosing to close that chapter. That chapter is over."*

*Be patient and compassionate with yourself. Forgiveness is not for the fainthearted. Console yourself and choose to be gentle. Give yourself what you need as you practice forgiveness.*

*"I am worthy of healing."*

*"I forgive others so that I may live a happier life."*

*"I have compassion for others."*

*"Everyone is doing the best they can."*

*Hawaiian o'oponopono: "I love you, I'm sorry, I forgive you, Thank you."*

*"Everything that happens to me is for the evolution of my soul."*

*"Everyone I encounter is for a divine purpose."*

CHAPTER 10

# Feeling

Most of us don't know how to feel. We're human beings with feelings, yet we're so caught up in our smart phones or the TV screen we've become experts at blocking out what's really going on. We're so used to numbing ourselves we've forgotten how to feel. We use various vices — drugs, sex, alcohol, porn, shopping. These addictions give us a temporary high, then it's back to reality. We indulge in these addictions because we need an escape.

We're usually less than fully present and when something happens bad to us (it can be anything), we quickly move on to something else. We live in a world full of distractions and it takes focus, discipline and courage to allow ourselves to feel, moment to moment. How often does someone piss you off and instead of dealing with it, you move on to the next distraction? How often do you push the thought out of your mind and pretend nothing happened? How often do you pretend that life is peachy perfect? I think we do this collectively. We're taught to live this way from birth. How often do we truly acknowledge and then release our feelings?

I'm not suggesting that when someone pisses you off, you go totally crazy on them. Ghandi said, "An eye for an eye makes the whole world blind." I believe you should express anger in a safe setting and in a respectful manner that doesn't harm anyone, the release it. You should protect your feelings, and if that entails standing up for yourself, then do so. This applies to all feelings: joy, stress, nervousness, excitement, rage, sorrow.... If you're not really feeling these emotions, you're not really living.

My grandmother is ninety-five years-old and she has hardly any wrinkles. They say, "Black don't crack," but I believe she's aging gracefully because she's living fully. When she's sad, she feels that pain and cries. She gives herself permission to feel the pain. A couple of days later, she goes back to her daily routine. It doesn't mean she forgot about the loss or painful experience, but she has truly released the emotion and gone on with her life.

She does the same thing when she's very happy. If someone tells her good news, she yells with joy, cheering for the other person. If something is truly funny, she laughs hysterically. If she is in physical pain, she allows herself to feel it. To be truly alive, we have to acknowledge our feelings. I wish people were encouraged to express their feelings more. Most of us suffer from suppressed feelings, because we think society demands it. I believe we should wear our feelings on our sleeves, shamelessly, passionately, confidently. The more you learn to trust yourself and connect with your intuition, the more you'll know how to interact with others. Let it out. Who cares what the naysayers have to say about you? It's your life to live, so why not live it fully?

Honor your feelings. You're entitled to them. They are an expression of who you are in that moment. Learn to give yourself permission to feel everything. Why not? Good and bad experiences are a part of life, so why not feel them? The sooner you let the bad ones go, the sooner you make way for the good ones. Feelings don't have to be good or bad. They are what they are. Don't sell yourself short by numbing your feelings because of fear thereby limiting your range of experience. Not allowing yourself to feel is the same as not allowing opportunities to come into your life. Remember the universal law that the energy you put out will return to you.

Society is constantly shoving consumption in our faces. Commercials show us what we should be doing with our time. Social media teaches us to mask our feelings. We live in a capitalistic world. The harsh reality of consumerism is "profit over people," as my childhood best friend Brax Tinkler puts it. And if you don't actively and conscientiously make the choice not to stuff down your feelings or mask them in your social media posts, you're like everyone else. The beauty of life is that no one has the exact answer. There is liberation in this truth. Choose to be free with your feelings and your unique way of expressing them.

Have you ever walked into a situation that made you feel really happy? Maybe you were with a group, and you didn't want them to look at you like you were crazy, but deep down you wanted to jump up and touch the sky because of all the emotions running through you. Look at kids. When they're happy, they shout and jump and lift their hands in the air to express their joy. When they're sad, they cry. If they stumble and fall, they cry. They're not concerned about who is around them or whether they'll be judged for feeling the way they do. They're not afraid that their feelings may be hurt, and they know that even if they are hurt, the feeling will pass. A new moment will come and so will a new feeling.

# Suppressed feelings fester

For a long time, I was afraid to feel pain because of the trauma I suffered growing up. I was afraid to feel the pain of my lover leaving me. I don't think I ever acknowledged it to myself or to others. I suppressed all those feelings. And when you suppress feelings, they fester into depression. The emotions you try not to feel don't vanish. Oh, no. They're hiding within you. That suppressed pain is worse than if you had allowed yourself to feel it in the first place. Your wound expands because it has no outlet.

Picture a pot you keep filling with spoons full of feelings. They build and build and build as you suppress them, and when they finally surface—kaboom! Your well of pain has run so deep that you feel all the pain ten times more. Sometimes twenty times more. Heck, maybe a hundred times more. Trust me, I'm speaking from experience and it's not fun.

The mega superstar I had dated really messed me up. He wrote a song about me that devastated me, not because of what he said, but because it was true. He wrote it when I was facing all my trauma for the first time, trying to put my life together, and unable to figure it out. My reality had shattered, and it felt like everything hit me ten-fold. Because I hadn't faced my feelings for the majority of my life, I kinda lost all my shit when they came up.

No matter who you are, you are human. We all bleed, shit, make mistakes, learn and grow. The megastar I was talking to was Lil Wayne and it was a life lesson for me. To be clear, this is not a flex, I'm only mentioning this because I want girls who fantasize about these things to understand that life is not all cranked out for what it seems like and because this is a part of my story, my authenticity, and my truth. Don't get me wrong, I am grateful for the person he is and the gift of lessons I learned by us connecting in this lifetime. At the time, while I liked him for him, and we had a beautiful bond, I was lost and did not value love for what it was. There are a lot of girls like that who don't **real-eyes** the true value of love and instead search for the wrong things. (If I could tell those girls one thing it would be to first know yourself and first work on loving yourself). I can now look back on this connection with gratitude but also compassion for myself. He ended up writing the song "How to Love." *You had a lot of moments that didn't last forever, Now, you in this corner tryna put it together.*

I couldn't start healing until I was able to face the feelings in the song.

# FEAR OF PAIN

In the book *F\*\*k it! The Ultimate Spiritual Way*," author John C. Parkin writes that we are only living in fear due to the fear of pain. But the minute we remove the fear of pain, we remove fear itself. Maybe something terribly painful happened to you in the past and now you're afraid something like that will happen again. Your fear has taken over, and you can't find peace or happiness. When people judged me for smiling a lot, I became afraid of smiling in public, so I didn't do it. It wasn't until I faced that pain and decided not to let it control me that I could be free to smile openly. If I hadn't been afraid of the pain, what people thought wouldn't have bothered me.

The book is fascinating because its approach is to say- Fuck it. I'm going to forget about the pain. Fuck it. What's the worst that can happen? Choosing to say, "Fuck it, I'm not afraid of no pain," liberates you. It reveals the limitless courage that is always accessible to you.

If something disturbs you, be willing to face your fear of pain. Take courage, you limitless soul, you. Acknowledge that whatever it is may hurt a little bit or a lot. But once you accept that and the moment passes, you'll be on to a new feeling and a new moment, ready to freely accept what life brings. You'll **real-eyes** that painful feelings are not that evil. Most of the time it's about cultivating compassion for ourselves and others. It might feel like a monster is trying to attack you.

Phillip Agnew, community activist and co-founder of the Dream Defenders said, "When I see my monster, I want to ask it what it has to teach me." Sometimes pain shows up to teach us lessons. By overcoming my fear of being ridiculed for smiling, I learned not to give my power away, and to understand that I have the right to feel happy. Who cares if others don't like it? I'm entitled to live my life the way that fits me best.

I'm here to tell you to feel, and to be proud of your feelings. Sure, every life includes some periods of pain, but once you accept that, you can **real-eyes** that pain is just one of the many emotions that present themselves to us. Acknowledge that pain is not going to kill you. Fuck it! Then you'll begin to learn the many lessons that come with every feeling.

# WITNESS YOUR FEELINGS

**Real-eyes** that feelings come and go. Something much deeper and much more truthful is under all the many feelings, and that something is you. Your divine being. You are in the midst of every joy and pain you experience. You are unencumbered, unbothered and still. According to the Vedanta school of Hinduism, the Atman is the true self, free of any influences. That self-resides in stillness beneath all the passing feelings. Your soul is infinitely more powerful than any feeling that comes along. Your soul witnesses the fantasy game we call life.

You can begin by witnessing your feelings as they come and go. Test your tolerance for pain. Challenge yourself. If something painful arises, instead of running away or tuning out, sit with it. You might be surprised at the solutions that come up. Feel it. Feel everything. Feel the excitement you get when you have a trip coming up. Embrace new moments. Feel them. Feel sad when you lose a loved one or if someone hurts you.

Nothing lasts forever. Everything is temporary.

# CHOOSE TO FEEL GOOD

Feelings come and feelings go. But dude, choose to feel good. When you feel good, your life gets better. It's not always easy but build the practice of feeling good. Let's say you wake up first thing in the morning, and you're already like, "Oh my God, not today. The day hasn't even started, and I feel like shit." Acknowledge that you woke up not feeling your happiest and find something to feel good about. Someone once told me, "You must be like me, we're the kind of people who like to wake up and just be happy." He was right, I am like that. Because I learned a while ago that you don't need anything to feel happy. You can just feel it for no reason at all. You can just be happy to be you. Think about the times when you've been happy. There hasn't always been a major reason for it. Some days, you just feel happy. Ride that wave.

You can find things reasons to be grateful —your health, the sun, a friendly companion. Just the fact that you can breathe and hear your heart beating. How about being thankful for the ability to be thankful? I saw a meme on Twitter that pictured a garden separated by a fence. On one side, a woman had lots of green grass and dozens of roses, but she was miserable. On the other side of the fence a woman had only one rose and no green grass anywhere, but she was feeling good! She was happy with her one little rose. Appreciate what you have. You can have nothing and still feel good.

You can choose to feel good about your life no matter how little you have. It's all about your perspective.

# ALLOW YOURSELF TO FEEL

Feel your negative emotions, too. They're here to teach you something. How can you feel positive emotions if you never allow yourself to feel the negative ones? A negative feeling may show you that you need to look at something, to step back and check yourself. It may be a signal to move forward with a change of direction. Feel everything, you precious soul, then let that feeling go. Too often, we run away from the "bad" feelings.

Men tend to do this most often because society has convinced them that being manly means never showing emotion. This may force them to shut down. But we're all emotional, and those who feel the need to hide their feelings the most are the most emotional of all. I believe men die at an earlier age and commit suicide more often than women because they have more stress. Can you imagine how stressful it must be to be taught not to cry, express your feelings, or be vulnerable? Yet vulnerability is actually strength. Some older men have hidden their emotions for so long the feelings begin leak out of them in the form of depression, regret ...

From a very early age, men are taught not to express their feelings. But dude, clearly that's not the most rational idea. Choose to let the feelings flow. E-motion is energy in motion. It's not meant to be bottled up inside.

When you allow yourself to truly feel, you become more alive, more passionate. Feelings are an expression of who you are. How can you live your life to the fullest if you don't allow yourself to fully feel? We may be reluctant to fully express our feelings because we're afraid of disturbing someone else's peace or of being judged. But, eh hem, whose life are you living again? If someone is upset because of how you feel, that's their problem. They need to tend to their own feelings. You are entitled to your feelings. Don't allow anyone to take that away.

A girlfriend of mine was interested in dating someone of the same sex. She didn't feel that way about other women, and didn't think she was gay, but she was attracted to this one woman. She was afraid of how her family would respond. So she hid her feelings, and didn't live her life fully from fear of causing them anguish. Eventually, she couldn't help being true to herself and went with the other woman, and they were happy. This sort of thing happens all the time.

Again, everything is perspective. By acknowledging your feelings, you allow yourself to be a passionate human being. I read a meme that stated, "The freest person in the world is the one who has nothing to hide." Choosing to feel is an act of courage. It means looking at what you may not want to see. And once you really see it, you may want to run.

I choose to look at feelings as a way of evolving. Even painful feelings are there to allow me to feel something. If everything felt good, how would we know what good actually felt like? If everything was perfect all the time, we might get bored. Sometimes, the bad happens so we can appreciate the good. All things, including feelings, are temporary. Be brave enough to be true to yourself, then move on to the next feeling or lesson waiting for you. Live from your heart as well as your mind. Your heart is your life force. Open up your heart, even when it feels the most frightening. I'm reminded of John Mayer's song "Say What You Need to Say." Feel your beautiful soul. Feel it as often as you can. Every moment you truly feel will last a little bit longer. Choose to relish them all.

# Practices/ Affirmations to Help you Feel

*Face the things that scare you the most. The more you do this, the more you will* **real-eyes** *that your thoughts are silly. What's the worst that can happen? Like really.*

*Challenge your fears through taking courage. Tap into your inner strength and choose to feel instead of running away, which is usually a cop out. Face what's happing in the present moment, feel it. It's going to pass and it will not kill you.*

*Live fully. Even if you have to push yourself to do so from time to time. Whenever she gets self-conscious about stepping out of her comfort zone or "society's comfort zone," my friend Jamie uses this mantra: "The only person you're trying to impress is you."*

*Practice self-awareness and positive self-talk. Notice what comes up for you during the day and talk yourself through it. Find out what's making you feel a certain way. Comfort yourself. Talk to yourself lovingly and give yourself what you need at the moment.*

*"I am worthy of all that life has to offer me."*

*"I take life in fully and with vigor."*

*"I fully experience the totality of what it means to be me."*

*"I have the courage to feel the things I may not want to feel, since everything is temporary, anyway."*

CHAPTER 11

# Letting Go

When you finally let go of the things that no longer serve you, you leave room for beautiful things to enter your life. I **real-eyes-ed** this truth when I finally let go of my ex-lover after four years of suffering. I hadn't been able to move on, because the men I met didn't measure up to him. They didn't have the money he had, didn't have the power. They didn't have the understanding he had, the personality, the charm, the smile. I didn't care what they brought to the table, but I was mad that I was still single. All I wanted was him. I dreamt he'd come back into my life. I couldn't accept life the way it was happening. I felt my dreams were shattered and I had to come up with a whole new life plan. Life happens, and we only have so much control. I was miserable in the love department because I wanted to be with him.

One random Sunday, I saw him from a distance and I could tell that he was in a very, very dark place, messed up on some serious drugs. I was disgusted. That wasn't what I wanted for myself or what God wanted for me. I told myself not to judge him but to have compassion for him. In that moment, something very beautiful happened. I was able to let go of him. I no longer clutched him to my heart. A huge weight lifted from my chest. I had been blocking other opportunities, so stuck in the past, I couldn't allow the new to come in. As soon as I released him with love, I opened myself to new people. Two weeks later, I got involved in a new relationship after being single for four-and-a-half years. I could let life flow because I'd finally let go.

I'd spent days and nights praying for help to let go of him, but I didn't know how. Sometimes, we try to force things before they're ready to happen. I wonder what would have happened had I not tried so hard to get over him, if I'd let things be and gone with the flow. One day I couldn't stop thinking about him, and the next day I stopped thinking about him altogether. One day I might feel like sleeping in and another day I might feel like being extremely productive. It's all okay. Try living without forcing yourself. Tell the Universe that you're okay with yourself and the flow of life..

Think about how often you're not okay and can't seem to float with the flow of life. If we don't try so hard to hold onto things, we can see that life is smooth sailing most of the time. Bad things inevitably happen, but how often do they occur? If we understand that we're okay most of the time, we **real-eyes** there's no reason to worry. With a little strength, faith and trust in the Universe, things usually work out. Yet we try so hard to control our lives, when really, we only have so much control. Decide to do things and then do them. It's simple. Trust. No need to overanalyze everything. How many times a day do you tell yourself Instead of saying "should" or "have to," try saying "I choose to…"… The idea of choosing is much more positive.

It's about learning to surrender to the moment. On her YouTube channel, Oprah posted a video called "I surrender it all." Check it out. She was out in a field crying, when she began singing a song to God called "I surrender." At that very moment she received a phone call from Steven Spielberg offering her a feature role in the film *The Color Purple*. Her message is that we are all co-creators, and that we should give up the idea that we can do everything on our own. When we **real-eyes** that we have a Creator who is much more powerful than we are, the source of our unique existence, we understand that it only makes sense to let go. Have you ever heard the phrase "Let go and let God?" There is so much truth in that. We can get so worked up trying to control things when the truth is that we cannot control everything. We have no control of when the sun rises and sets. Don't force it. Control what you can, when you can, but relax. Let God have His way, too. And **real-eyes** that it's okay to trust the Universe. It's not that scary.

Nature flows. Nature is never in a rush to get somewhere or do something. Nature is always at ease and takes life as it comes. We, on the other hand, are constantly analyzing what happened yesterday, or fearing what the future might bring. If you've visited the Caribbean islands, you may have noticed that the people are super chill. Sure, they get work done, but their attitude is much cooler than that of the average American. They stop and say, "Hi, how ya doin?" "Everything cool?" "Everything irie?" It's the culture, the way people flow with life. They're not constantly trying to control everything. It's as if they truly understand that what will be will be and what they can control, they will when the time comes.

# BE FULLY PRESENT

Try going a week without struggling to take control of every element in your life. Learn what contentment means. Practice letting go for one week. Eat when you like when you like, and it will probably be a well-balanced nutritional diet. Because once you've had too much chocolate, you will naturally start to crave green beans or whatever your body lacks. When you practice contentment, you'll sleep when you like and wake up when you like, and it will probably be just enough for you to be well rested. Sing when you want to sing and dance when you want to dance. Talk to whoever you want to talk to and stay quiet when you don't feel like talking. To anyone. If you feel like crying, bawl your eyes out. Then dry them and go on with the next moment.

Learn how to be fully in the present moment. You can't be fully present if you're still holding on to what just happened. Nor can you be fully present if you're worrying about how you'll pay that bill on Friday. I'm not suggesting that you avoid necessary matters such as bills, but don't dwell on them so much so that you're not living fully in the present. Enter each new moment without baggage.

Only when you fully live in the moment can you be totally liberated and become one with clarity, creativity, divinity. Only when you live in this new moment can you fully feel the sun basking on your skin, hear the children laughing from their souls, focus on your work in a place of limitless creativity, truly feel gratitude and what it does to your spirit. I can go on and on trying to describe the mysticism that arises when you choose to dwell fully in the present moment, but you should experience it for yourself. You'll notice a freedom from the past, a weightlifting, because you are no longer burdened by whatever was disturbing you. You'll feel that anything is possible, because it is. Anything is possible if only you believe, but half the time, we're so lost in our thoughts we don't fully grasp what's going on right now. Gently remind yourself to be present. I try to remind myself often. Remind yourself because you want to, because you're tired of living in your head. I promise that life is better in the present moment.

I invite you to be fully alive! It's as simple as that. Drop into the moment and let the fear go. Most people are living dead lives, imprisoned in their own minds, confined by fear or regret... You deserve to live the richest life possible. And by rich I don't mean financial wealth; money can't give you the truly rich life you deserve. I'm talking about a life free from pain. A life where you are free to fully be you. Where you are free to fully listen to whatever or whoever is around you.

Whenever we were at parties together, my friend Kathy mingled with everybody. She said, "I just go wherever my soul feels comfortable" Be like Kathy. Go where your soul feels comfortable.

Live in the now, not in your mind. Love is never so real and rich as it is in the present. Love is an action. Bask in life's beauty in the present and go where your heart tells you. Allow yourself to be free in this moment. Allow yourself to feel good. Let go of all the other shit. If you're restless, surrender to it. Give into love.

If you feel like learning something new, learn it. If you feel like cooking, cook. If you feel like feeding the homeless, do that. Scream if you feel like it. Watch TV all day for once. Follow your own rhythm. We are confined by thinking we're supposed to behave in a certain way. How does that make sense if we are all created differently? We express our unique feelings in our own way. Why on Earth would we hold back those feelings? Or thoughts? Or actions? Do we risk looking stupid? Man, fuck all that and just be. Does it look like animals worry about what others think of them? Are they concerned with how they're "supposed to act?" Heck no! Animals are chillin'. Observe them. You could learn a thing or two.

Nature sustains itself effortlessly in a cyclical pattern. Look at the cycles of the seasons, of the sun and the moon, the constant flow of beginnings and endings, transitions, transformations. Take time to really savor the emotion of gratitude. Hold onto the moments when you fully experience beauty and love. Keep those feelings inside you and let go of everything else.

# DROP INTO WHAT IS

I took a magic mushroom trip with my very spiritual friend Jamie who was always curious about the mysterious and had an interesting take on things. She brought along a book titled *The Psychedelic Experience: A Manual Based on the Tibetan Book of the Dead* by Timothy Leary. Dr. Leary wrote about the therapeutic benefits and positives spiritual effects of mushrooms, and he clearly explains how to view life and let go. That experience allowed me to completely let go of fear, with the help of Dr. Leary's guidance and Jamie's companionship. I was completely open to the way the Universe wanted me to react to this altered state. I was confident it would be a positive experience because our intentions were sacred. It helped that we both consciously chose to stay in a good mood.

I was carrying a lot of heavy emotions at the time. A tree called me, and I tried to connect with it, lying back against the trunk and resting my feet against the roots. I dropped my shoulders. I had so much pent-up heaviness from the trauma of losing Kamden. I was still carrying around a heavy load of grief, down to the cellular level. I had been in a deep depression for a couple of years, and there was a lot of residue. I found a friend in that tree and as I leaned against it, I felt love. I felt safe. I felt like the tree was giving me the biggest, warmest, most comforting hug I could ever imagine. I was free of all fear.

The sensation took over my being. Jamie had just read aloud Leary's admonition to let go and drop into what is, and I was able to do that. I dropped into what was and gave into the tree, and the tree embraced me. It purged me and poured all my gunk into the ground. I began to feel much lighter and at ease in a state of bliss. I got into a deeper state of connection to my self-love, as well. I believe that the mushrooms had opened my heart to receive the message of Leary's book, so that my state of mind shifted, and ultimately, my state of being.

I was able to really connect with Pachamama, Mother Earth and give her gratitude for that beautiful moment and day. The experience taught me a life-long lesson. It taught me to drop whatever I no longer needed. Pachamama will take it and recycle it. That's what it felt like. Mother Nature is so intuitively intelligent that it naturally recycles things back into the earth. Nature is there to cleanse us when we need a little help letting go. We don't have to do it all by our lonesome selves. We can turn to the spirit world for assistance. Don't forget that you are not just a physical body and a mind, but you are also spirit and soul.

# ALLOW THE MOMENT
# TO UNFOLD

Every so often, I find that I'm able to drop into that state of letting go again. Think about how often you feel anxiety. Pay attention to how many times you feel worried, stress, angst throughout the span of a day. Trust me, you're not alone. When these feelings come up, use them as a cue to start letting go. Allow the moment to unfold. Do what you intend to do but be aware of what's going on around you. The more you practice this, the more often you'll be able to let go.

Wouldn't it be great if we could take a few moments every so often to drop the heaviness we drag around and get rid of that built-up stagnant energy? By dropping our heaviness not only do we become lighter, but we also let go of more and more fear. The more you let go of that fear, the more you are able to trust. The more you trust, the more open you are to co-creating with life. The more open you are to joy, to yourself, and to life.

One night I met a young Caucasian lady who wanted to wear her hair in dreadlocks, but was afraid of what others would think, especially in her workplace. I wore dreads for a year and a half. It was such an empowering experience! I felt beyond free. It was definitely a symbolic experience, and locs come with the gift of wisdom.

Some refer to them as an antenna that picks up signals from the spirit world. If your soul is calling you to start a loc-journey, go for it. That means your soul wants to communicate with your most authentic self. That goes for anything your soul craves. Your soul will always lead you to positive things. Listen to that voice. It's you leading you to yourself.

# Practices/Affirmations to Help you Let Go

*Surrender your heat. Choose to give into the things beyond your control, and to trust.*

*Give yourself the opportunity to drop into the moment. Drop into the taste. Drop into the sound, the feel... Let go of fear and worry moment by moment.*

*Allow yourself to feel good. This coincides with letting go.*

*Dance. Do things that make you let go. Maybe it's a late drive, the beach, skydiving. Maybe it's a new meditation class. I know from my own experience that meditation helps liberate us and allows us to let go.*

*Let go of the expectations others have of you.*

*Let go of perfectionism.*

*"I am going with the flow."*

*"I am relaxed in every single moment."*

CHAPTER 12

# Optimistic Reggae

Years ago, I heard an upcoming soul artist sing a song called "Optimistic Reggae." He said he'd been inspired to write it by his uncle's battle with cancer. It was a reminder to stay strong during the hard times. You can find it on YouTube here: https://www.youtube.com/watch?v=SXY-jA6eLgo.

The lyrics go like this:

*"I let this optimistic reggae be my guide. I look up at the stars. I let the sun shine down on me. Life is too short. All you've got to do is smile."*

We can choose to relate to life as optimistic reggae. Even when things go badly and it seems impossible to get through them, we can look up at the stars instead of looking down. We can choose to be optimistic.

There is an ebb and flow when you choose optimistic reggae. Ever notice the way reggae's slow dub beats soothe you? The music is therapeutic. Studies have shown that the slower deep beats of the base in reggae reduce stress levels. Reggae is chill music that flows through your soul. I'm sure some of Bob Marley's greatest hits have made you feel better. "Don't worry about a thing, every little thing is going to be alright," Or "One love," or "Redemption Song." I think optimistic reggae taps into the mysticism you can sense when you quiet down and pay attention to the subtle flow around you. No matter the chaos that may surround you, you can tap into the mysticism of optimistic reggae.

When you look beneath the surface of good days and bad days, you'll find an ever-present silence. A great speaker once encouraged his audience to tell themselves "I am a rock star." Then he asked them who just said that? Try it yourself. Your pure, rock star bliss is always there, under the surface. Optimistic reggae means living in love. It's the feeling you get when you're not afraid, when you are not living in angst or worry. It's an essence you can tap into that shows you the beauty around you. Whether you're driving, at work or at home, you can choose to be aware of the life around you, choose an optimistic perspective, and tune into living in love. Choose to believe that you are in perfect alignment, aware of synchronicities as they occur. Choose to relish the good fortune that shows you it has your back. Believe the Universe when it reminds you that you're right where you need to be, no matter how terrible your life may seem at the moment.

In her song "Beautiful," Carole King wrote, "You've gotta get up every morning with a smile on your face and show the world all the love in your heart. Then people gonna treat you better. You're gonna find, yes you will, that you're beautiful as you feel." It's up to you to choose your perspective on life.

# GIVE YOURSELF LOVE

I recently moved to a new state where I don't know many people, so I'm making friends as I go. In this small college town, it's difficult, maybe because there are so few people my age. Maybe I'm overreacting, because I've been here less than a month. I was getting a little, lonely and blue. When I got tired of being depressed, I switched things up a bit. I decided to substitute my loneliness with something better. I decided to give myself the love I longed for.

Why not be jolly, even on the crappy days? Remember that you're always where you need to be. Whatever you're going through is teaching you something. We may not know what the lesson is, but trust that it's for your highest good. Thank the experience and let it go. Maybe the experience will help you become more optimistic, maybe it will reveal something you don't know about yourself. Maybe the experience will make you stronger. Strength doesn't just appear like magic. It's developed by overcoming adversity. I believe we each have an infinite amount of strength within us that we can tap into. It's always there but we have to learn to reach for it. Like building muscle, you need to work out your inner strength to become stronger.

I find the best way to build strength is by being optimistic. This morning, I was worried about money, and it was slowly but surely putting me into a funk. So, I chose to get excited about the day. Why not? I was like, "Fuck it, let's go up from here." I chose to talk to God. I chose to find things to be grateful for, like a good lunch, or like the jolly guy who rang me up at my supermarket. Little things.

Many times, when tragic events occurred, I felt I had no choice but to be optimistic, to learn how to wear a smile even when I felt like dirt. I had to try to overcome the demons, to tap into a higher wavelength. During my pregnancy, the baby's father decided to leave me, just when I needed him most. Was I hurt? Absolutely! It was one of the most difficult times in my life. A girlfriend asked me why I wasn't crying every day. She said I was handling it very well.

I said, "There are tons of weak bitches out there doing it. So why can't I? I've gone through enough bullshit to know that I can get through some rough patches along the way." It is all about perspective and how you let something ruin you or strengthen you. It is what it is, man, you only have so much control over your life, so might as well look at the bright side and make the best of it.

# PUT THOSE GOOD VIBES OUT THERE

It's easy to fall into slumps. We've all had moments when something feels disastrous, even unbearable. Why do some people handle difficult situations better than others? Why do some people allow problems to defeat them while others face the challenge head on and overcome it?

Fear defeats us more than anything. But fear is an illusion. It's "False Evidence Appearing Real." Strangely, when people feel pain, they become even more afraid. You're already feeling the pain. Use the pain as an indication that you need to make a change. Don't be afraid that the situation may get even worse. There's always hope. Always. Take courage and face the pain dead on. Look at the pain and choose to be happy. Nothing will change in an instant, but something powerful happens when you choose to be happy instead of sad. You find ways to push through pain and move on over to joy. It may be as simple as declaring that today will be better every morning when you wake up. You'll be happier today than you were yesterday. As hard as it may seem, challenge yourself to find a way to be happier, because you are so over the pain.

Being alive is like going to war. with yourself. Will you cave-in or will you fight? Will you spend your time laughing or crying? Recently, I spoke with a stranger about spreading love in any way possible, whether it's through visual art, or singing, or writing a book. Put those good vibes out there and serve others. You'll feel better. A man said that he was a stand-up comedian, and that all his life, when things got tough, instead of crying, he made others laugh.

# BE THE LION,

## NOT THE MOUSE

I'm not suggesting that you pretend life is always peachy and repress negative feelings. No. I'm suggesting you face what may come, good or bad, but smile and hold your head up high. Fight rather than squirm or run away. Instead of getting lost in your feelings, force yourself to focus on something inspirational, such as a video, or music, or a friend you know will uplift you. We all have positive tools available to us. Use them. If you look around, you might see a positive message in the form of a sign from the Universe.

I recently went through something that felt unbearable, and I felt like giving up. Every morning when I woke up, I thought, "Oh this again!" Reality was so painful, I wanted to sleep all the time. But going through the experience taught me so much! It taught me that I had to fight for my happiness and my health. I had to fight for my heart. And I'm still fighting through it, but it's getting better because I am coping better. My thoughts are optimistic and that allows me to have hope. I'm learning that life will get better one day and that it's really not that bad. I'm finding a strength I didn't know I had. Not until we're faced with great challenges do we become great.

Difficult experiences force us to find ways to make our lives better. Have you noticed that so many people are posting uplifting messages on social media? Why? Because they make us feel better. Painful experiences are opportunities to learn how to fight, to fight for happiness. No one on Earth wakes up happy every day without having fought to get there. When I went through a terrible breakup with an ex and felt alone and horrible, I could either choose to stay miserable and become bitter, or **real-eyes** that I could fight to feel better. I knew I might not feel better when I woke up in the morning, but I resolved to smile five times that day.

Practice fighting for happiness by getting out in nature, go for a hike or chill at the beach. Try solitude. You may feel crappy and have a million thoughts going through your head, but at some point you'll feel grateful you're there. Try listening to music all day long and ignoring everyone in the world. Call a few close friends, not to talk about your own depressing situation, but to listen to them. Focus on things outside yourself. Feel happy for someone else. In the midst of your misery, choose gratitude. Find something to be grateful for every hour of the day.

This fight for happiness shows you that you are powerful beyond your wildest dreams. When you wake up every day ready to fight for happiness, you will begin to **real-eyes** that you're gradually becoming happier. You may feel terrible all day, but in the evening, you might **real-eyes** you're feeling kinda happy. And maybe, just maybe, the next day you'll wake up still feeling happy. Maybe later that day you'll feel depressed again, but now you'll know you don't have to be sad forever. You'll continue fighting to be happy because you've seen that it's slowly but surely working. Happiness requires constant effort. It's not a state you reach once and for all, but it doesn't take much to **real-eyes** it's always there under your misery if you choose to do the work.

Courage, faith and hope will pull you through the tough times. You'll develop these traits as your fight continues. As you refuse to be defeated by sorrow, you'll get stronger within your being. Finding happiness is like climbing a rope. It's a struggle to get to the top. No one is waiting on the other side of the rope to drag you up. You have to make the choice to be happy yourself.

Chances are you'll be inspired along the way. One day I was in my car, waiting at a stop light and feeling crappy when I noticed a homeless man wearing brightly colored clothes in the crosswalk. I threw up a wave and a humongous smile and gave a thumbs up to the car beside mine. The smiles on all sides were infectious. This moment of random joy taught me to smile, and not worry, be happy. I often remind myself of that moment when I'm feeling down.

Life isn't a battle against other people. They're in school with you, learning lessons just like you are. Don't hate someone who does something terrible. Thank them. They're your angels, here to show you something or send you in a different direction. You, however, are here to love and to learn.

# FIGHT FOR HAPPINESS

Finding happiness is a personal thing. Only you know what your unique happiness looks like. We each have our own way of deciding what's good or bad. If two people experience the same trauma, one may heal while the other may become bitter. Experiences are just events. How we react to them is up to us.

Happiness comes from within. You could be at a carnival with loved ones and be miserable. Or you can be in the midst of a fight between loved ones and be at peace with yourself. It's all about perspective. Choosing happiness is an action. It's a decision to make the most of every moment.

Without optimistic reggae, without hope, courage, and strength, you will be defeated. No one else controls how you think, how you feel, how you behave. You may be feeding the source of fear. Have you ever been in so much pain, you were afraid you'd never feel joy again? I'm here to tell you to fight with all your might, to look for the light beyond that pain and fear. When you're struck in darkness, you have the opportunity to choose a different way of being, a way that will bring you up. You may be seeing darkness, but you can CHOOSE to see the light. The next time something difficult or unpleasant happens, bring your guns out. Grab the bull by both horns and ride the shit out of it. If you fall down, get back up and ride it even better. And keep riding until you've overcome the situation.

Remember that everything changes with time. Your current situation will pass, but while you're going through it, you have an opportunity to build strength. Don't let life get the best of you. Challenge it and show it what you're made of.

I've faced huge challenges and built character along the way. It's easier to sulk in your sorrows, but when you choose to stand up and fight, to focus on the good things in life, you become powerful. Your problems no longer have power over you. You have chosen to take power into your hands and to own it. By choosing to be happy in the midst of all your worries, you build character. You weren't born to be a little weakling who gives up on life easily. Use your power to the best of your ability. You were born to use your higher intelligence and evolve. You were born to love your entire being. Never allow yourself to act like the coward you weren't meant to be.

I don't believe that any of us were born to crawl under a cave and hide when life got hard. Try to be strong in the face of challenges big and small. You will soon **real-eyes** that there is no actual limit to how strong you can be. I believe we all have what it takes! Build your strength until nothing can really phase you anymore, because you've overcome so many trials with joy. You may be faced with even greater challenges, but you'll have resilience, a better reaction to pain and sorrow.

# HOLD ON TO JOY

Happiness is a treasure to be cherished. People may think you're crazy for being so happy, but never ever let that change you. This is YOUR life. Stay true to the joy you've worked so hard for. No one can give you joy, and you deserve it. Never let go of it. We all know too well what it's like to be unhappy, but few of us know true happiness. Yet you can carry happiness with you throughout your life and beyond.

# LOOK ON THE BRIGHT SIDE

Let's take another look at optimism. If it rains all day Sunday, look at the bright side. You can catch up on those movies you've been wanting to watch, or finish writing that blog entry. You can be cozy all day. Maybe somebody cuts you off while you're driving, and you crash into them. You were about to trade your old beaten-up car for a brand new one, anyway. Maybe your love has left you, but that helps you **real-eyes** that he or she wasn't the one you were meant to spend your life with. The more you keep building this habit of optimism, the easier it becomes to stay optimistic when something unwanted happens to you. It becomes a switch you can turn on whenever you need a little more light.

Life will continuously present us with unwanted situations, but we can change our perspective to believe that everything happens for a reason. We can choose to welcome all things in life. We can make a conscious choice to feel good no matter what, to be bright in a world where people tend to look at the dark side. Look around at those around you who may be lost in their own minds, caught up in worry about what could have, would have, should have happened. You can see their miserable thoughts written all over them. Dude, be different! Be who you were born to be and trust that that is AMAZING. Feel good and be happy! Trust that there is always a bright side and choose to look at it.

**Kam-Bridge:** When I gave birth to Kamden, I had the choice to find ways to stay positive. I could choose to be grateful for my precious moments with him. The sound of his voice. The way he called out to me. No matter how bad life gets, you can always find something to be happy about. I was happy for all the outings we took with him, for how chill and good he was, how sweet and caring, for how much personality he had. I knew when he had an attitude and when he missed his mommy. Knowing that my time with Kamden would be short helped me to make the most of every moment. So did the difficulties I'd experienced in the past. I spent many years during my childhood trying to figure out how to look at the cup half full. Everything I had gone through prepared me to handle this. If not, it wouldn't have happened.

# SMILE MORE

Celebrate life even when you think there's nothing to celebrate. Dude! Celebrate your health, your legs, your voice, your presence! Try this for a change: smile. I'm not saying walk around smiling all day long but try smiling more. I've never seen anyone with an ugly smile — even if all of their front teeth are missing. There's something magic in a smile. Not only is it contagious, but it's also beautiful! It's a language everyone can understand, and it emanates positivity! It releases endorphins that make you feel happier. Try it.

I was lost in my head all morning overthinking things, until a stranger complimented my smile. I said, "Thank you. I need to smile more!" In that instant, I **real-eyes-ed** how beautiful smiles are and how beautiful we feel inside when we smile. When I smiled, I was no longer caught up in my worries. After the man complimented me, we exchanged a few more smiles and a laugh. I call that good vibes. Bob Marley's son Ziggy wrote a song that goes like this: "*Keep giving me that good vibration. It's giving me that inspiration.*" Good vibes are truly inspiring.

Next time you see the cashier having a crappy day, smile. Next time you're having a crappy day, smile. You never know when you'll brighten someone's day. The person who receives your smile might need it more than you imagine. Maybe your soul needs it more than you imagine. When you make the effort to smile, you're healing the part of you that felt weak and broken. One smile at a time, you're healing the wound inside you. You're cracking some sunlight into the darkness. Whenever you smile at someone, even if they don't smile back, you're shining sunlight on them.

Dude! That's not all. When you smile a lot, you age better! You see the accumulated stress on someone's face as they get older. Whether we frown or smile a lot, we mold our faces. I don't know about you guys, but I want to age gracefully. And aside from how beautiful smiling makes us on the outside, it makes us that much more beautiful inside. A smile is like wearing a name tag that says, "I am happiness. I am positive. I am light! I am *optimistic reggae*." Genuine smiles shine from the inside. Smile baby, just smile.

# Practices/ Affirmations to Help you Live Optimistically

*Make time to take in all that's around you through breathing, looking at the colors around you — or heck— smelling the roses. Slow down and use your senses. This makes it easier to focus on the good things.*

*Live a life with hope. Know and understand that there is always hope, no matter what the situation at hand.*

*Look for the pros more than the cons. Choose to look at the cup as half full, not half empty. Remind yourself that "at least its... thank God it's not... I'm happy this taught me... I'm grateful for..."*

*Use your bad mood as a signal to start being more positive. It can be a cue to consciously choose to start feeling good. Like, fuck it! You already feel shitty and it's not making anything better, so you might as well force yourself to start feeling good. Give yourself a push. It will build your inner strength.*

*Make Bryant's song a daily mantra: "All you gotta do is smile... optimistic reggae, optimistic reggae."*

*"I am focusing on my personal happiness."*

*"I am worthy of being happy."*

*"I chose to focus on the positives."*

*"Happiness comes from within."*

CHAPTER 13

# Dancing with God

When I mention God, I'm referring to the Creator, the Universe, Jah, Abba... whatever you choose to call a Higher-Power as you understand it. I believe this God is happy. I will always believe we are all meant to be happy, but that without sadness, we would never know what happiness is. I believe that heaven is a state of mind that can be found here on Earth, the same way that hell can be lived on Earth. Every day I see people who look like they are living in straight up misery, like they're living in hell's dungeons. I know that thousands of people in the world die of hunger every day. Someone is always suffering much more than we are, but we still sulk and complain of the horrible things that have happened to us. Usually, these things have occurred in the past, and nothing too terrible is happening at the moment. Even if you're reading this in the hospital suffering with pain, know that this moment will pass, as well. We walk around like sad zombies stressing over our "horrible" pasts when plenty of people would gladly trade your past for their present.

On the other hand, some of us are making the best of our lives and the best of the present moment. Hello? Hip, hip, hurray! That bad moment from the past is over. Can you imagine if all the bad things we felt lasted forever? Now, that would be horrible!

This may sound a little hippie-dippie but look at how positive the world really is. We are so conditioned to thinking things are horrible that we believe they really are. Man, I don't care how bad you think your life is, it's full of beauty, full of laughter and love. Just sit back and consider how much love and support you truly have. Let's say you're one of the many people in today's world who feels alone. I'll bet the smallest gesture of kindness means that much more to you. There was a time in my life when I felt very, very lonely and the simplest thing could make my heart melt. It might have been a random text message from a friend wanting to wish me well. Man, during that time when I felt I had no one, that message meant a thousand times more to me. Watching a little girl smile made my heart melt. I may have a tender heart, but I appreciate those things. They may seem little but to someone who feels alone, they can be important.

# LIFE IS FULL OF LOVE.

I promise myself to always hold on to the wonderful feeling of being supported and loved and to always remember that I'm never alone no matter how alone I may feel. To remember that life is full of love and that the Universe loves me abundantly, because the Universe is abundant! Has the Universe ever provided for you when you least expected it? I'm sure it has; The Universe has surprised me many times with what I needed when I least expected it.

**Kam-Bridge**: When I was pregnant and abandoned by the father of my child, I felt I had no one and I didn't know how I was going to make things work. I could count on some family members, but I couldn't rely on them for everything. To my surprise, God provided me with the most support I have ever received. I was given a beautiful baby shower with about forty people in attendance, and I received everything my son would need. I was showered with more gifts, love and support than I could have imagined.

At another time in my life, I needed money to pay friends who had let me crash at their place until I got my life together. They hadn't asked to be paid for the use of their sofa, but I had to give them something for the utilities until I found a job. At that time, I had nothing. Then one day, after praying to God for help, I walked to the nearby Starbucks with a bible in my hand. As I was waiting in line, the guy in front of me said, "That's a good book, isn't it?" I smiled and replied that it was. We began a conversation, and he told me about his life and how the Lord/Universe blessed him abundantly. I told him nothing of my troubles. We didn't exchange phone numbers, because he made it clear that he wasn't approaching me that way. All I got was his name, David. As we parted, he said, "There's a reason I am supposed to give this to you. Don't even thank me, the Universe will reward me ten- fold. I just feel called to give this to you." He handed me a one-hundred-dollar bill. I'd never met him before, and I'd told him nothing about what was going on in my life. I was in line to purchase something, so how would he know I was in need? Boom! The Universe supported me through him.

At times when I thought things wouldn't work, they did, and I began to trust that they always would. I promise to dance in this place called my life, because, man, life is truly a blessing. Every day that I wake up healthy and free of pain is a blessing. People out there are struggling for real, man. The spiritual leader Ram Dass once said, "God is the dancer, and you are the dance." I find that very beautiful.

You can become conscious of God's presence when you are acutely present in the moment. You not only witness but feel a flow, an eternal warmth that lies underneath, always. And because you are in the midst of this flow/dance with God, you are in bliss. You taste eternity. In those rare, rich moments, you may ask yourself, "Where did I come from? Where was I before I was born? Where will I go after this life? Why is my soul here now? Who am I?" Or you may simply feel incredibly alive. In those moments, you are with God. Each of us defines God in our own way, but when you are conscious of the present moment, you begin to dance. You begin to feel your limitless power with all your senses.

This may happen when you travel to somewhere new, and you're stimulated by all the new sights and feelings around you. You're free of the everyday concerns of life. This may happen when you're feeling good. I'm all for feeling things, but do you really think God wants you to be sulking every five minutes? No! If the Universe wanted us to suffer all the time, we might as well have been born in hell.

# LIFE MAKES SENSE.

God wants us to be happy. Look at the Universe around you. It looks happy. Consider the clear blue skies, the puffy white clouds, the cool breezes that graze your skin no matter what part of the world you're living in. Sometimes it rains and sometimes there are natural disasters, but the Universe always recovers and replenishes itself, and in the process, there is beauty. Consider the soul of the Universe, the being that lies beneath the surface of all that we see. There, too, you can find beauty. When you see that life makes sense, like a jigsaw puzzle coming together, you **real-eyes** that the Universe is working with you and doing the dance for you. You are simply dancing along with it. Change is always going to happen, whether you like it or not. Give in to the wonders of the Universe.

Try to surrender. Try to give in to every new moment as though you're watching a film. You're the lead actor, but you're also the director and the audience. If you can see your life from this perspective, you'll have a clearer identification with self and a healthier interaction with life.

We are born, and then what? This new life has an expiration date, but we have so much to learn as we make the journey. So much to experience. So much to give and to receive. We have ourselves to explore and learn to love. We have a whole world to experience. I may hate whatever is going on in my life at the moment, but the great news is that life goes on, and in a few hours, night will fall, and then a new morning, a new moment and a new experience.

Within a year, we will all be new versions of ourselves. There is liberation in this knowledge. Things are constantly changing, and this is exciting news because it means we never have to take a single moment too seriously. Dude, life is bliss, and the Universe is positive energy.

# THE UNIVERSE IS ON YOUR SIDE.

The Universe will reflect your energy. Put out positive energy and positive experiences will come to you. Once you make that a habit, you'll feel good more often. Life will become sweeter. You'll dance to a better song, move your soul to a better rhythm. It's about allowing life to flow and trusting that the world is not so bad, that the Universe is on your side. Even when things seem to go wrong, it's about trusting that there's an important lesson to be learned. It's a surrender to what is, an unfolding of your soul, letting it come undone by stripping away the layers you've covered yourself in. It's **real-eyes-ing** that the world we live in is beautiful. It's choosing that perspective. I'm not suggesting that you ignore all the horrible things going on in the world. But I'm asking you to choose the perspective you want to live with.

Only you live in your mind. Only you can choose how you view life. Why not choose the brighter perspective that things will get better, that just maybe, if we all had a brighter perspective, we could transform the world and make it an even more wonderful place? Maybe things would seem easier, more pleasurable.

Someone recently told me that I've been running away from difficulties all my life and that I'm addicted to the easy route. If it's hard, I want no part in it. I said, "It's not that I want to run away."

A lot of things in life are hard. There is no way of getting around the fact that you have to work for things. But I do tend to choose the easier route, because I don't think life has to be hard. It's all about perspective. If I don't like the way something feels, I have the right to leave. If we all chose to look at life with ease and decided life wasn't so hard, we would be incredibly strong. Nothing would seem too hard to get through. We wouldn't turn to drugs, alcohol, and partying, trying to escape life's hardships. Life would be a treat, not something to dread or just get through.

# EMBRACE LIFE'S MYSTERY.

Have you noticed the culture here in America? Most people are walking around like life sucks! Like it's so terrible. Look at people in any grocery line. You may find those rare few who choose to make their day bright by conversing with the cashier or the person in front of them, but most people live every moment as though life is horrible. Look at the pain in their eyes, the stress on their faces as they wait at a red light. Look at the way people mistreat others so effortlessly. You see this every day. It's rare to find someone who is excited about life and the unknown.

Life is a mystery. We don't know why we're here, where we come from, or where we go when we leave. But we know we're here. Embrace that fully. Welcome the mystery of life and the unknown of it all. Embrace the fact that anything can happen at any moment, and it probably won't be bad. Tough one to absorb, huh? It's so easy to think something bad will happen to us because we're so used to our lives not going as planned.

Nah, life is a treat, and anything can happen. I don't care whether you're rich or poor. Experiences that may seem small to you might seem huge to someone else. Those childhood experiences you hated so much made you who you are today. I can almost guarantee they were necessary. So, let the burdens go and dance with God, Allah, the Universe — whatever name you choose to call the Higher-Power behind the curtains of this play known as life. You can dance in the moment within yourself. You can do it right now. It's a dance between you and God.

# DANCE WITH GOD.

Cultivating a relationship with the Creator of the Universe makes life that much better. Embrace change because, I promise you, it will always be knocking on your door. Embrace it because you are all you have, and you will always have yourself. You will spend all your time with yourself, so you might as well enjoy it. Express yourself, because if you don't, are you really dancing? Face your insecurities and fears and you'll find the confidence that always resides within you.

I don't care who you are, you're beautiful. Your soul has beauty. Your heart has purity. You were born as love. You owe it to yourself to find the love that resides within you. What I'm suggesting isn't simple. It takes work but you can change your perspective and look at it as easy. What's too hard for you to do? Think about it. We are divine, immortal souls. A Higher-Power created you just as you are. Whether you believe that you are that Higher-Power or that there's something greater out there doesn't matter. Dance with God because you are a god, because you come from God. That is your heritage.

Practice appreciating the simple things in your life. You may find they bring you great joy and love. Practice incorporating all the chapters of this book in your life. Do whatever feels right for you, but most importantly, love. If you feel fear, love. Whatever that means to you, love.

When I'm most afraid, I know that I need to feel love. When I feel resentment or anger, I need to love. In every moment, I can consciously choose love. That's what feels right to me. Ask yourself what feels right to you? There is no wrong answer. Listen to your soul. Your soul will show you how to evolve.

## ONE LOVE.

## XOXO.

# Practices/Affirmations to Help you Get Closer to God

*Pause and envision that you really are dancing with God. You don't have to give the source energy a face but do experience getting intimate with it.*

*Allow yourself to feel good. Let go. Apply the tools in the previous chapter and really allow yourself to taste the nectar of life's sweetness.*

*Trust God. Trust it all. Might as well. What do you have to lose when you'll lose it all eventually, anyway?*

*Physically dance. However silly, however your body and soul want to move at the moment.*

*"I am one with God."*

*"The divine source lives in my center."*

*"We are all one."*

*Pray and beg God to get closer. You will see a shift in your relationship with God.*

*The relationship between you and the Universe is proactive and mutual. It's about walking in faith, knowing that something so much greater is supporting you because you trust it to do so!*

CHAPTER 14

# The Silver Lining

When you go through something huge, something tragic or monumental there's always a ginormous lesson and hopefully, a transformation for you. A ginormous shift. These big, tragic things happen to help your soul evolve, to make you discover something within yourself, within your life, or within the universe. It might cause a personal revolution. It's a treasure underneath the tragedy, a gem to take with you for the rest of your life, even though it might not seem that way in the moment.

Hopefully, one day you'll understand why things happened the way they did and how they have changed you for the better. I don't think tragic events happen for no reason. I don't think the Universe is that cruel. All of nature is constantly evolving, so why wouldn't that be the case with you and your journey in life? Trauma changes us. If it's intense enough, and we survive it, it changes us forever. The intensity of trauma remains in the body, and that energy needs to be expressed. Everything within your being has been rearranged on every level: physically, mentally, psychologically, spiritually, and emotionally.

When Kamden was first diagnosed, a social worker told me, "Vanessa you will never be the same again. You can't go through something like this without changing." I was like, no way! Me? I thought I was solid in who I had become, but I was wrong.

I had been brutally beaten by life in those two years, but I wasn't defeated. No, not with this soul of mine. The amount of strength I had to pull out of my soul blew my mind. The amount of power, determination, hope, courage and faith I needed to get me through was out of this world. Of course, I'd changed. Of course, life required a part of me I didn't know I had. And if I hadn't found that strength, I might as well have died. The experience showed me that we're limitless beings. I needed an enormous amount of strength to survive. I needed it to come out on the other side.

# ACCESS YOUR INNER WARRIOR.

If you think your life is so bad, try getting through something like that. If others can get through worse, so can you. Having survived what felt like a big ass typhoon, I became stronger. Through determination, willpower and courage I found the inner strength I possess and I'm grateful for all I went through. I feel confident that I can get through anything that dares to try me. I can run circles around anything else that may come my way."

This is a strength I want to always possess. You never know when life will ask you for everything you've got. You'll wanna be able to access your inner warrior. That warrior is yours alone and won't look like anyone else's. Maybe your inner warrior comes out while you take long healing baths. Maybe it comes out by practicing awareness, or by getting into your zone while bike riding or jamming to your favorite tune. Whatever it is, you can access that warrior by connecting with yourself. See how you connect to your warrior the next time you need it.

A lot of my strength came from my Godfidence, my confidence in God, in my Higher-Power. Someone once stopped me in Runyon Canyon, one of the biggest tourist attractions in Los Angles, and asked me if I believed in a Higher-Power and why. I told him I'd hit a point when I felt I had lost everything, so I might as well believe in

God. Might as well have faith in something, right? When you have nothing left to lose, you have everything to gain. I had to believe that there was something more, that what happened didn't mean that my life was over. He was like, "You mean, you just force yourself to believe in it?" And I was like, "Yeah. It is what it is. When you believe in God, you've already begun to believe in what you can't see."

Those of us who know the power and presence of God know that it's real. Choosing to tap into the force of the spiritual means going beyond the limits of human capacity. It's Godfidence, of the God essence we all possess. When I saw the word "Godfidance" floating around Instagram, I knew exactly what it meant. It's relying on a supernatural confidence; it's feeling confident because God is with you.

I met a grieving mother who had lost her nineteen-year-old son and told her, "Well, that isn't as bad as being homeless." Her response was, "No, this is worse, Vanessa. I'd rather have my son alive with me and be homeless."

Once you've hit rock bottom and survived, you can survive anything. You don't have to let life's challenges destroy you. No, fuck that. You didn't come here for this! Nah, you weren't born to be defeated. You came here to end up on the better side of the spectrum and never let anything get the best of you. Choose to let everything that comes your way make you better.

I came here to be a conqueror. A warrior. I came here to be victorious. And so did you. We really are capable of being un-fucking stoppable.

Before I lost Kamden, I'd never lost a loved one. One day while hiking, I happened to overhear a man telling someone, "I don't handle death very well." And I wondered how I'd be when I experienced it. Would I handle it well?

Even in my wildest imagination, I'd had no idea how hard it would be to mourn Kamden's loss. I'd become used to him during the sweet months we had together. Our bonding was so intense, so freaking beautiful. We understood each other on a level that's hard to describe. I'm his mommy, and a natural attachment is part of a mother's deep love. It's almost inconceivable how much good a mother wants for her child. When that child is physically taken away from her, it's unbearable. The pain is so excruciating it seems impossible to go on living. When I lost Kamden, my world shattered. I didn't know how to be okay. I completely lost it many times.

One morning I was on the phone with the bank arguing about waving a fee because of what happened. I had already gone into detail about losing Kamden with another teller and when I was asked to go through it all again. I started coughing and sighing, huffing and puffing. I said, "Are you serious? That is so fucked up!" I hung up and started screaming crazily. I needed to release so much steam. It's one thing if a teller says they'll wave a fee for the next few months and forgets. But I'd told her I'd lost my son and was struggling to find a job, and she hadn't bothered to note that on my file. You never know how your actions may affect someone. Especially when it's your job to serve them.

Man, I screamed with all my might, and I started crying. I had countless episodes like that. I had to yell it all out, scream, cry in public. It was way too much for me to bear, so I snapped at people, which is really not my character. But at the same time, I was learning to stand my ground. That day, after I yelled and released all that, I said to myself, "I am not going to allow this to control my emotions. I have fought too long and too hard to let this ruin my day."

# KEEP FIGHTING.

For a solid eight months after Kamden passed, every day was a struggle. After fighting so hard for my sanity, I refused to let someone's laziness ruin my day. How someone chooses to treat me has nothing to do with me. People choose how they act, and we choose how we react. We're in control of a lot more than we think we are. I chose to fight, because the last thing I'm ever going to do is to give my power to someone else.

My spiritual being and physical body felt exhausted. I felt trampled, depleted. But here's the thing: I was aware of a constant feeling of defeat. Life was brutally beating me, but I never allowed myself to get knocked down. I kept fighting, even when I was on the floor. I fought with all I had. No matter how bad the lows got, no matter how dark the hour, I kept fighting. I thought how defeated my son must have felt enduring seizures every single day, breathing with a tube in his nose and down his throat. But he was a rider. He didn't let anything get in the way of being alright. He was able to stretch, relax and exude love like nobody's business. That taught me I had to fight, too. Man, if he came here for such a precious sliver of time and fought like the champ he is, then I had to give it my best and fight, too.

I got up every fucking day with my emotional fists up and

my self-confidence intact, my inner strength building. I was determined to never, ever let life defeat me, no matter how grim things got. I believed I was a warrior. I've heard that "the fight after the fight is the hardest." I found this to be true. When Kamden was diagnosed with a fatal disease that was hard. But after he passed, having to search and dig for every ounce of fight within me was harder. Having the endurance to go on and never give up on myself required the most strength.

When we fight to do something consistently, it becomes a habit, a life skill and a new reference point. a craft we can master and use in the face of difficulties. Who wouldn't want to have more fight in them? Life isn't for the easily defeated.

Fighting has taught me many things. The strength to fight is always available, if you search deeply enough. And when you're really in a fight, you need support to make it through. That can be a local support group, inspirational quotes, it can be family and friends who stick around through a rough patch. For me, the greatest support comes from the Heavenly Father. Or Mother. The Creator. As it says in the Psalms, "God is our refuge and strength." And "I can do all things through him who gives me strength."

I know how tragedy can make you mad that God allowed such a thing to happen. But maybe it happened to bring you closer to Him and, ultimately, to yourself. Maybe it taught you how strong you truly are, that nothing can take you down. Maybe it took you to a deeper place of self-love. If God is truly loving, it must have happened for a reason like. Maye the pain polished the diamond of your soul just a bit more. It's so important to see the good in it all, even if it seems like an unending quest.

I had to incorporate faith in my fight. I had to believe that something greater than me was carrying me, and that I would win this fight. I had to believe that moment to moment. I had to believe that I was not alone. I was blessed with a few dear friends who supported me and a supportive family who helped me out whenever they could. But many in my support group lived in other states.

Thank God I found a supportive therapist. It's crazy how the Universe sends you the right people, as though they were destined to walk with you at that time for a specific reason. I will be forever grateful for her precious spirit and for every soul who walked hand in hand with me during that journey.

The therapist, Samantha, told me, "When you first came to my office eighteen months ago, Kamden had already been diagnosed and you said, 'I need help getting through this, because I don't know how I'm going to do it.' You were using your voice to get what you needed. Whether we **real-eyes** it or not, we all know what we need and we make sure we get those needs met. And you did."

I took the steps I needed for a healthy recovery. But I felt alone. My grief was too intense for other people to understand, and I think a lot of them were afraid of it. Sometimes I wanted to remind them that I'd just lost a son. But I accepted that they had no way of understanding what I was feeling, and I was grateful for their support. When I say my family came through, they came through! They taught me what family really means, and I can't thank God enough for choosing the best team to be my family members. I feel very fortunate that such loving, thoughtful people knew how to be a rock when I came tumbling down. I pray that one day I can show them my appreciation by giving back to them.

My best friend Tiff was the second person I told when Kamden passed. Her immediate words were, "Do you want me there this weekend or for the funeral?" She and so many others showed me what a friend is and what friends do. I asked her if she could come that weekend. All of it meant the world to me. My family helped me organize the funeral arrangements, and my friends flew out to support me. I led the way as my friends carried Kamden's casket.

Although I'm grateful for the support I had after Kamden crossed over, at times I had too much pain and I turned to faith to help me believe I'd make it through. It's almost funny how we can be so caught up in our problems that we allow them to consume us all day, and it may be something as miniscule as "I need more money to make ends meet this month." Or that someone at work is getting under your skin. Anything might be bothering you, but it isn't until life really hits hard that you see those things weren't such big problems in the grand scheme of things. It's interesting how the tougher times can really bring us closer to God, to source energy. My own experience brought me the closest I've ever been to God.

A few months before I became pregnant with Kamden, I was planning to move to L.A. from Miami, and I dreamt I was in Africa. I have yet to visit that continent, but the dream was so vivid, I could smell and almost taste the air, which had had a very distinct, dusty scent. First, I was on a very busy street with crowded markets. Then I was in a deserted area with three men, two of whom were clearly against the other one, who was dressed in an army uniform. One of the two men took out a sword and sliced the army guy's hand, then ran off. I ran up to the guy with the sliced hand and asked, "What are you going to do now?" He said, "I'm not going to worry about it." Then he looked up and pointed to the sky. He said, "He's going to take hold of my hand." And for some reason, I knew he was referencing God.

At the time, I had no idea what that dream meant I just thought it was bizarre, to have dreamt that when I was about to move to L.A. The craziest part is that I usually open the bible to a random verse after I ask the Holy Spirit to lead me to the place, He wants me to read. Over and over, I found bible verses, mostly in Isiah, that stated, "I will take hold of your hand." I didn't know what that phrase meant for me, but I decided to declare, "Okay, God, you're going to take hold of my hand."

That first summer in L.A., I had Isaiah 41:13 tattooed on my forearm as a reminder that God will always hold my hand. Later, I needed that reminder more than I could have ever fathomed. That verse helped me get through my walk after Kamden passed. It helped me feel secure in the knowledge that I was not alone and that He was holding my hand through it all.

Hebrews 11:1 is very powerful verse. I repeated it to myself over and over: "Faith is having confidence in what we hope for and assurance in that which we do not see." I could not see the end of the tunnel. I could not see the top of the ginormous mountain I was climbing. What I did see was that I would make it through. Daily, I had to convince myself of this truth, to make myself believe it. I talked to myself like this almost all day, trying to lift my spirits. Whenever doubt entered my mind, I chose to combat it with my faith in the Holy Spirit. I placed my faith in a very powerful entity whom I could not see but in whom I entirely believed. I believed I was never alone. Not for a split second.

Partly because I was so terrified of being alone, I forced myself to believe God was there with me, and that I would not be solely responsible for carrying myself through this. He would be holding my hand every inch of the way. I became very well acquainted with the Divine Being, our Higher-Power. I considered Him my very intimate best friend. When I felt like crying, He was there. When I felt a moment of joy, He was right there with me as I cried tears of joy or felt gratitude in my heart. I say "He" as in an energy presence — source energy. I felt full, knowing I was blessed with Divine Protection.

Events in my life have clearly attested to this. But now I **real-eyes-ed** that God truly does have my back. He has all our backs. It made me **real-eyes** that whatever we may go through, He is always there. If we cry, He will be our shoulder. If we ask for strength, take my word for it; He will give us the strength we need if we ask for it.

I could not have gotten through losing Kamden without my faith in God. I think I would have ended up on drugs. I was already suicidal. But God's spirit kept telling me, "Keep going. Don't stop." Dark forces were trying to take me under. I kept meeting the wrong kinds of guys, the wrong types of friends. I sometimes found myself in dangerous situations where I was offered drugs. A kingpin asked me to push weight for him across country in an eighteen-wheeler. Had I not had a strong foundation in my faith in God, I don't where I'd be right now.

# IN YOUR PAIN, YOU CAN FEEL YOUR STRENGTH.

I've become intrigued by my capacity to get through anything. You always have the choice not to give up. Now that I am on the other side of my pain, I have been transformed. It came down to building faith within myself and in something greater than myself. We can find relief in knowing that so long as we live, there will always be new moments to come, and that there is always space for transformation and evolution.

Finding the silver lining helps connect you to your spirit and the purpose for your journey, but it takes a lot of love from within. It takes courage to find something positive in the midst of overwhelming negativity. It takes so much courage to be kind when you're going through hell. It takes love to see the beauty around you and pick yourself up again. We live in a world that can seem dark and trying, but I have discovered that if you push yourself hard enough, you can find joy.

Own the love that drives us forward to see a new day. If you keep fighting, I promise you will start to see the good. It will become a habit and, eventually, a new way of living. We're capable of getting through anything if we fight hard enough. We're capable of thriving. We have the capacity to get better and better. No matter what.

I thought, "If I die, I'll see God again, reconnect with the source energy. So, what is there to fear? We're all divine, infinite beings."

# LOVE CAN NEVER BE DESTROYED.

Although Kamden has come and gone, our loved ones never completely leave us. He may no longer be here physically, but his energy goes on. My bond with him has only gotten stronger. Even after a loved one passes, we can still keep a strong and beautiful bond with them. We're all spirits, too, you know. Science says that energy can neither be created nor destroyed. And we are energy.

In his book *I Am That*, the guru Nisargadatta Maharaja wrote, "We're never born and we never die." I had the craziest conversation with a guy who goes by the name DJ A-OH who broke the guru's theory down this way: "At our most basic level, we are electrons, protons, atoms. We reincarnate consciousness when there are enough of the right atoms. But if atoms never die, and we are one hundred percent atoms, we never actually die."

I badly wanted to get a tattoo of the Asian proverb "All is illusion," which implies that only love is real. All that's not real will eventually disappear, but love will never leave us. We are all made of love which can never be destroyed. It is so pure. When all this is over, only love still exists. The love Kamden and I shared, and still share, was so big and it will always be just as big. That didn't fade a speck. If anything, it's transformed into a deeper bond. When our loved ones cross over and transition to the other side, we are blessed with very close guardian angels.

See, Kamden was special, maybe too special for this realm called Earth. He has the majestic essence of a king. He was always protective of me. I could feel it. He still is. And for this, I truly feel honored I don't physically see him, but I love him just as much. We go somewhere after we die. Our souls are truly eternal. We don't simply die and that's it. Poof! That's the end of our souls. No, our beings are infinite, and deep down, our souls know this. Even after we die, our souls are very much alive. I like to tell Kamden that I'll see him soon. Because if we really are infinite beings, I will. This makes me fear death much less. It takes some of the pain away. It's "I'll see you later," not "Goodbye." I live with the love Kamden and I eternally share at the forefront of my heart. It was the most genuine love I've ever known, so why let it go? I choose not to. I choose to connect with our love every day because it's beautiful.

Our bond is not only stronger now, it's active. I've decided to open my mind to the idea that life does exist after we leave this Earth, and that we can always connect with the energy source of someone we've lost. If we allow ourselves to be open enough, we may be surprised at how close the relationship becomes with a loved one who has crossed over. Kamden communicates with me in different ways. Like the way we had our own language of "hmmm, hmm." He comes to me in the form of a white butterfly, and I feel his presence close by. It happens almost every day. The love that transpires in this type of exchange is the purest I have ever experienced. As I write this sitting on my porch, I see a white butterfly fly by in front of me.

Kamden passed away one month after my thirtieth birthday. I was thirty years young on this planet, and I transformed so much in a very short time. One of my best friends told me that Kamden turned me into a new person. He was a soul who taught me many things. Most importantly, he taught me unconditional love. He taught me to get closer to God, to use my voice and really own it, vulnerability and all. The experience taught me how to stand up for myself and put my foot down when I need to be assertive. It taught me to believe in my soul. I'm not sure I had much of a choice when I was in survival mode.

The experience took everything out of me, all the emotions, all the heartache, all the love that felt like it was piercing me. I felt I was being converted into something entirely different because of the intensity that was going on. How close can someone be to letting it all go? I felt as though I hit every tipping point. One day in the future, I will be able to see how all this has shaped me into the person I am becoming. One day, you, too, will be able to see how all the events in your life have shaped you into who you are today. What I now know is that the person I am today is way different than the person I was before Kamden came into my life.

I've always been spiritual, even as a kid, but since Kamden passed,

I've been diving into spirituality more and more and deepening my practice of it. For now, I need meaning in order to live. When you lose someone so close to you, you see how precious and short life really is, so it's natural to feel the need to live with greater meaning. You see the world through a new lens. The experience steered me in the right direction, and now I propel forward with greater purpose. Losing him has made me try hard to do the best I can do with the time I have left here. He came here, but he didn't get to have childhood, a graduation, a long life...

I have created a foundation in honor of him called "Kamden's Room," which runs an ongoing effort called the Smile Campaign. The goal is to bring smiles to children by donating books and teaching them guided meditation. Kamden's Room is not a physical place, rather, we go to children, especially in underprivileged schools, so they can have a chance at a higher literacy rate. These are things that Kamden was not fortunate enough to have in this lifetime.

There really is so much to be grateful for, so much to give back. You don't have to lose somebody dear to you to go out there and make a difference. There should be no excuse. Even if you have a little, you can still give back. You can still do good for others. You can still do something meaningful in this world.

Our time here is precious and can be very unforgiving. All you have is right now. What are you going to do to make your time on

Earth better, not just for yourself, but for others? Are you going to leave a legacy for the generations to come? Why in the world wouldn't you? I **real-eyes-ed** the experience of learning not to give up has helped propel me toward all my goals: physical, mental, spiritual, personal, emotional and professional. Now if I ever feel like giving up, I remind myself of the song I used to sing while trying to get through it all: "Horses don't stop, they keep going."

These little reminders help me stay motivated to keep striving for nothing short of the best. I take way better care of myself now. The experience turned me inward and made me build a very intimate relationship within myself. I **real-eyes-ed** the more I connected with myself, the more I connected with others, with nature, with the Universe. The more I **real-eyes** I am connecting with myself, the more self-love I feel.

# CONNECTION IS LOVE.

If you feel connected to yourself, you feel self-acceptance, which leads to self-love. People who accept you fully as you are help you believe in yourself more. Some people are naturally accepting they make everyone around them feel that they can believe in their authentic selves. Loving yourself and believing in yourself are parallel emotions.

I could go on and on about how much the experience — all my experiences — changed me and shaped me into the person I am today. Because I pulled through, I feel like nobody can tell me shit about myself. Knowing that I got myself out of some real-life boo-boo, shows me what I'm made of. I have a reserve of self-confidence because I have seen that whatever I put my mind to, I can do. This Godfidence in my inner strength lets me know I can face anything in life. It tells me that I can chase my dreams, and that nothing is impossible, that nothing will stop me unless I allow that to happen. After all that I've been through? Hell, fuck no! I didn't come here for that. I came here for a reason.

The day Kamden passed, as I held his cold body in my two hands, the same hands that held him the day he was born, I felt something for the first time. I **real-eyes-ed** that this would be my outcome, too. It became very real to me that we are all going to die.

Fact. So, I can't give a damn. Can't give a damn about what others think, or how they may judge me. Someone insecure will always be busy judging others. I can't give a damn about my fears, because at the end of the day, none of that will matter. I know damn well I'll have to face myself on my death bed, by my damn self, and I wanna be happy with the life I chose to live. I wanna know that I lived with meaning. With purity. With grace and authenticity. I wanna know that I gave back to others, in whatever form, big or small, that I gave it my all. I don't want to have regrets. I'd rather chase my dreams till death than give up on myself. I don't have time to play games. I didn't come here for that. I have a calling, and if I don't follow it, I won't be true to myself. I'd rather die trying. At least I'll be getting somewhere.

There is a calling inside each of us. If you don't know what yours is just yet, you'll find it eventually. The Universe has designated a path for you. You may choose from many routes, but you need to follow a path that is aligned with your heart. Dive deep and ask yourself what you're living for. What do you want to be living for? How do you want to be living? Are you happy with the way you're living? What can you do to make yourself happier?

I used to think the end goal was happiness. Everybody out there wants to be happier. But happiness is temporary, as all emotions are. It's not the answer.

# FIND THE STILLNESS WITHIN.

I'm discovering that it's about contentment. I think back to the times when I've experienced highs, and I've experienced lows and something was witnessing it all. This goes deeper than the joy you may feel in the midst of something great in your life. Say you just got married and you're in the honeymoon phase. Life is amazing, right? But underneath all that is something more that never leaves, something that has been with you from the beginning. I'm finding that what is more important than being caught up in finding happiness for myself, is making sure that the stillness within me witnessing it all is content. It's about being content within myself. This goes for all of it — adversity, devastation, stress, excitement, celebration, change... Can you be the stillness in the midst of life's dances?

No matter what's going on in your life, good or bad, that stillness, which is really your soul, is always the same and never changes. That stillness is your journey and the essence of love, the essence that resides beneath fear, sorrow, happiness — beneath all our emotions. Making sure that my soul is content is more important to me than chasing after fleeting happiness or instant gratification. Have you noticed that whenever you attain a goal, you go on to the next thing? If you just slow down and watch it all unfold, you can connect with that stillness within you.

I teach yoga and I tell my classes that "the stillness in the middle of the discomfort is the real yoga. The stillness in the middle of the bliss is the real yoga." Can you be still? I love meditation. because the more I practice it, the easier it becomes for me to get to that place of stillness. Silence has energy, a power that doesn't have to yell its lungs out in the middle of the room so everyone will notice it but is controlled and infinite. It is your true God essence and cannot be destroyed.

Life is all about evolution. If you're not evolving, you're wasting your time. You could be learning something new. You could be improving yourself, chasing your dreams. In the process of self-transformation, you evolve into a new person. You undergo a rebirth. At some point in our lives, we all go through these rebirths. It's just a matter of being open to the changes that inevitably occur. The Universe is going to do its thing. So, why the heck not make the journey a little bit easier and dance along with it? Choose to make each moment a fiesta.

My friend Tiff said it perfectly: "It's a choice you make every day when you wake up." I learned this early but forgot as life went on. When Kamden crossed over, I had to relearn it and apply it. Many people had opinions. They'd say I was too sad or too happy. But Tiff told me, "Ness, they just don't understand that you're naturally a happy person." I chose to feel and grieve in my own way. I chose to heal in my own way on my unique journey. When it was time to let the sunshine in, I ripped my heart open for it. Joy is always there if we choose to tune in to it. You can open your soul every so quietly to the present moment, to a subtle and reverent bliss. The more you do that, the more you feel it.

Tiff was talking about learning to be happy by choosing to live in the moment. And the crazy thing is, happiness is inside us always, even during challenging times. Think about it; observe it. It's always there. It's the same bliss you may feel when you're dancing. It's the bliss that was there before you were born. Choose to align with that energy. This is the power that gets you through everything and is always with you.

There's always a silver lining, a positive side to every situation no matter how hidden it may seem. when someone gets murdered or diagnosed with cancer, you may wonder how this can be true. Maybe it was that person's time to pass to the other side. Maybe that person's cancer was a lesson in fighting or taught them to count their blessings. I once heard that when someone gets stricken with something potentially terminal, it's because their soul is being questioned. They are being asked if they are willing to fight for life a little bit more.

I love life with all my heart and soul. It's full of buoyancy and laughter and surprise, and let's not forget to mention the lessons. After meeting Kamden, my life permanently changed for the better.

I appreciate life so much more. They say that happens to us when we hit rock bottom. We're much more grateful for the happy times when they come along. I'm not here to sell dreams and act like everything in life will always be peachy. I saw a gentleman prancing around whose demeanor and the look in his eyes made him appear to be homeless, although his clothes and shoes seemed clean and new. I could tell he was in a state beyond distraught. I told him, "It's going to be okay." And he replied, "I think so." I said. "I know so." He was able to respond positively because deep down in his soul he knew it was the truth.

We all have hard times. We may even have times when we feel we've hit rock bottom. I've found if you connect to your soul, you can tap into an infinite well of strength. You can connect to Source energy, which is always right there within you.

# Practices/Affirmations to Help you Focus on the Silver Lining

*"It is my right and duty to focus on my happiness daily."*

*"With everything in life, there's always a bright side."*

*"Look for the blessings in disguise."*

*"If nothing else comes out of it, transformation will."*

## CHAPTER 15

# Transformation

*I am nothing that has happened to me. I am present,
conscious awareness. I am not a victim of my past,
but a victor of today and my future.*

I'm still smack in the middle of my personal transformation/ rebirth. It's taken a few years, and I don't even recognize myself physically or internally. Every single day, I feel brand new, a more evolved version of myself. I never thought I would leave L.A., but here I am, living in Boulder, Colorado after spending seven months in Takoma Park, twenty minutes outside D.C.

I don't really care for partying at all, which is a shocker for someone who used to bottle serve in Miami Beach, and party on the stands of DJ booths every night. My interests are mostly spiritual, wellness, and positive living. I do a lot of yoga. I teach yoga, and I've started a healing practice. I recently got a tattoo on my forearm of Kamden's face on the image of baby Buddha. Even if I have a family one day, he will always be remembered as being a part of it and can be recognized and honored by his brothers and sisters.

I'm currently in grad school, something I would never have considered before Kam. I'm working towards a master's degree in Resilient Leadership, which merges sustainability and social justice. I told myself that if I went to grad school, I would simultaneously follow my original calling to learn shamanism. When I was twenty-one-years-old, a yogi dressed like a monk offered me a free hour-long palm reading. He told me that I was a shaman and that I had no other choice, that shamanism was my path. I had no idea what shamanism even meant, so I didn't listen and just kept living my life. A few months ago, I was taking a mediumship class regularly and was surprised to discover that a lot of information is coming through me. One day in class, we did a blindfolded practice and when one woman took off her blindfold, she started laughing. She told me that she'd picked up on a past life regression, and that in another life, I'd been an Indian shaman man on the West Coast.⁻

I had already decided to move West to study shamanism, so I didn't think this was a coincidence at all. After Kamden left this realm, I began telling myself that maybe I should follow my calling. I investigated shamanism and read about real shamans who had callings and what happened when they didn't listen. They might be tested or experience a form of initiation through life really messing with them. Some have been electrocuted or had near-death experiences... Some who chose not to listen to the call have become terminally ill.

Since I've been in Colorado, it's all been happening very quickly, which was my intention. Once it finally hit me that shamanism was what I should be doing with my life, I didn't want to waste time. The studying, the clients, the impact I've had on them, and the plant medicines I've discovered have been rich aspects of my life.

Although most plant medicines are not legal in America, I have participated in secret ceremonies involving the holistic, medicinal plants used by the indigenous people of the Amazon. Primarily, I have been working with mambe (powdered coca leaves) which is considered a feminine spirit that you make love to in a sense. This is the purest form of coca mixed with vital vitamins, minus the chemicals. You don't sniff the green powder, but let it rest inside your cheek. At the same time, you work with the masculine spirit of ambil (tobacco paste concentrate) to ground and balance the energy. I have also been working with wachuma (San Pedro cactus,) which has been a very loving plant ally.

Of all the plants I've been blessed to work with, the most powerful and beautiful is Ayahuasca. It's incredibly healing, but it doesn't solve all your problems. Rather, it shows you what your problems are so that you can do the healing work yourself. I completed a deep Ayahuasca dieta — dieting on a master plant — for specific healing in isolation, while participating in Ayahuasca ceremonies every other night for deep healing, possibly the deepest form of healing. Finding a shaman with integrity is crucial. Shamanism has become so popular in South America any Joe Blow can call himself a shaman and a false shaman can really hurt people. I was fortunate enough to find an authentic Shipibo tribe in Peru. Their family organization, called ShipiboRao, is the real deal.

With all plant medicines, it's vitally important to understand that they deserve and require deep reverence. The way they are used in ceremony must be respected and they must not be abused. It is crucially important to have excellent intent when speaking of these things. It's not okay to tell friends, "Dude! I just got back from this super cool ceremony where everyone was fucked up!" That is not what this is about. It's not about getting fucked up. It's about making love to the plant medicines and being in relationship with them so that they can work through you and bring you healing. These medicines are some of the most powerful and potent healing modalities in the world, so they must be revered.

These medicines will call you. They're here to show you your shit, to be the mirror reflecting what you need to work on in your life. Do I think I'm transforming? Yes, but I also believe that Kamden transformed me, that life transformed me, and that I'm still transforming. Life will constantly transform us, if we allow it to. You can choose to be closed off from all that is offered you through the grace of the Universe. Living in this technological world can make it easy to ignore the jewels of transformation that are constantly presented to us.

People may shame these plants by calling them "drugs." The physical sensation may be feeling "high" or "drunk" but that's not what they're about. Shamans warn against focusing on the sensations in the beginning of most traditional ceremonies and guide you to what's really important. It's about being open to medicine and what it has to teach you. It's focusing, tuning in to what the sacred medicine has to offer you. It's hard to consider any of these plants drugs. They force your body to purge toxins, so it's not about getting high, but getting well.

There's nothing glamorous about the experience. Most people purge and puke and are forced to look at the horror in their lives, which requires some serious courage. Most of us avoid the things we don't want to face by browsing through Instagram, Facebook, taking photos, shopping and pretending our lives are perfect, looking for a quick fix from external gratification. The true answers always lie within, deep within our souls.

I've also evolved in self-respect. I didn't always respect myself. I was raised without a father, and I needed guidance, direction and protection. I've been celibate for one year and three months, and I've decided to wait until marriage. I **real-eyes-ed** that I was giving myself away too easily. Not just sexually, but in every way. And if we don't honor ourselves and our worth, we're disbursing the internal jewels that are meant to be cherished. Take back your jewels and honor them. No matter what your past entails and no matter what others think of you, deep down, you know who you truly are.

Lately, I've been giving myself permission to be vulnerable. I have **real-eyes-ed** that with great vulnerability comes true transformation. If you allow yourself to move past your comfort zone and get to the crux of what is going on within, you evolve.

On my journey, I have come to love all my scars and wounds and I wouldn't want to be anywhere else. I have found self-compassion, and without compassion for self, we cannot know compassion for others. I have found kindness, gentleness, peace, power, and solitude.

All day long, I fill up on positive energy and affirmations. When I catch myself being unloving or unkind to myself, I immediately change it up and begin positive affirmations. In this way, my being can become filled with light and love energies, the highest frequencies there are. At the same time, I release all energies that no longer serve me. This constant dialogue is truly a high energy conversation between Higher-Self and self, and I begin to strengthen my spirit and my soul. I am beginning to become truly confident. I am far from perfect and I am ever-transforming.

**Some of the affirmations I'm using now are:**
- I respect myself and others.
- I am humble.
- I bring my power back and stand confidently in it.
- I am confident in my soul.
- I radiate light and love in every single moment.

When you fill your being with positive vibrations, it's difficult for anything negative to stay. Negativity will naturally leave your presence and it will be easier to heal yourself- to love yourself. Our society has been broken due to a lack of self-love. We cover ourselves up with anything possible to make not looking a little easier. Our economy thrives on consumerism, which is in direct proportion to lack of self-love. They dangle things in your face that temporarily fill the void. You think the name brand, the bank account or the title makes you more than you already are. I think we chase after these false values because deep down, we know that we're so much more than just human beings. Deep down, we suspect that we're immortal; divine.

We're gods and goddesses made from the same stuff as God. We are Earth. We are infinite essences. We are all made of stars. So, it only makes sense that we're lost in a maze, searching for the next achievement to validate ourselves, but the answer isn't out there. Look at what social media is doing to everyone. We're experiencing jealousy and insecurity at a collective high. Many of us are miserable. We don't know what our purpose is.

The answer, dear one, is in looking within. It's honoring the soul and understating what it has to communicate with you. Even if it doesn't feel so good. Even if it hurts, and there will be times when looking within will hurt. It takes abundant courage, but I believe we all have it in us to transform. I believe we all have the courage to look at our deepest wounds and admit that it hurts, to tell ourselves "I've got you. This doesn't define you. I will comfort you." We've got to kiss the wounds. We've got to love on ourselves.

Man, you've got to give it your whole heart. Rip your heart open and dive into the nectar of your soul's calling, dive into everything that makes it flutter. Dive into yourself and unleash your soul. Chase after your heart's desires, damnit. Don't quit. Don't stop for even a minute except to rest, love, and more love, then get back to it. Our time here is short. I know it's easy to think you'll live forever because we're so used to the familiarity of our loved ones, but that's not reality. Everything and everyone has an expiration date. So, what are ya waiting for, dude?

I wish you many blessings, a life of love and intimacy with your soul. If you don't achieve anything else, achieve a connection with your soul for it will change everything in your life. When you tap into your soul, you tap into infinite possibilities, infinite potential. And you will be aligned in perfect, divine centeredness.

Take what you like from this book, what feels right to you. My guess is, you're going to take whatever you're meant to take. You'll take what you need to help you on your path right now. I hope that you embraced your moments with me, that you embraced this book and all its positive intentions for you!

# Practices/Affirmations to Help You Transform

*"I am worthy of being the best version of myself."*

*"I am not afraid to look at the things I need to change to be a better person."*

*"I allow myself to be vulnerable."*

*"I listen to the callings of my soul."*

*"I choose to go where I am not usually comfortable."*

*"My wounds are a part of who I am."*

*"Even the most beautiful diamonds in the world have imperfections."*

*"I am unfolding more and more of who I truly am."*

*"I love me for me."*

# Meet Vanessa

Vanessa found herself at a fork in the road after her son Kamden transitioned over, but still committed to finding her true inner self and real strength. An M.A. in Resilient Leadership with a focus in sustainability and social justice followed, as did new sources of hope and energy. Today she is an empowerment coach, public speaker, and leader of feminine healing circles.

She is a living vessel of her multi-raced, Haitian spiritual roots and now fully accepts her calling as a shaman. Her sense of duty allows others to see light illuminate their paths in life through her tarot and mediumship. All the while, she has the empowering words of Napoleon Hill and transformative trips from the heart of the Peruvian Jungle resonating deep within her.

Vanessa is at home in sunny LA, embraces yoga, eats well, and spends time with her Frenchie puppy.

Made in United States
Orlando, FL
02 November 2023